The Reference Shelf™

Urban Planning

Edited by Andrew I. Cavin

The Reference Shelf
Volume 75 • Number 4

The H. W. Wilson Company
2003

The Reference Shelf

The books in this series contain reprints of articles, excerpts from books, addresses on current issues, and studies of social trends in the United States and other countries. There are six separately bound numbers in each volume, all of which are usually published in the same calendar year. Numbers one through five are each devoted to a single subject, providing background information and discussion from various points of view and concluding with a subject index and comprehensive bibliography that lists books, pamphlets, and abstracts of additional articles on the subject. The final number of each volume is a collection of recent speeches, and it contains a cumulative speaker index. Books in the series may be purchased individually or on subscription.

Library of Congress has cataloged this title as follows:

Urban Planning / edited by Andrew I. Cavin.
      p. cm.— (The reference shelf; v. 75, no. 4)
    Includes bibliographical references and index.
    ISBN 0-8242-1022-0
    1. City planning—United States. I. Cavin, Andrew I. II. Series.

HT167.U7276 2003
307.1'216'0973—dc21

2003053804

Cover: View of Chicago skyline and Lincoln Park. © Vic Bider/ Index Stock Imagery/ Picture-Quest.

Visit H.W. Wilson's Web site: www.hwwilson.com

Printed in the United States of America

Contents

Preface

As anthropologist Claude Lévi-Strauss remarked in *Tristes Tropiques*, the evolution of cities is a complicated and awe-inspiring process—the point where nature and artifice meet. "A city is a congregation of animals," he wrote, "whose biological history is enclosed within its boundaries; and yet every conscious and rational act on the part of these creatures helps to shape the city's eventual character. By its form, as by the manner of its birth, the city has elements at once of biological procreation, organic evolution, and aesthetic creation. It is both natural object and a thing to be cultivated; individual and group; something lived and something dreamed; it is the human invention, par excellence."

Urban planning is a professional discipline, one that originated in the early decades of the 20th century, largely as a response to public concern over the deteriorating social and economic conditions brought on by industrialization. What began as a loose affiliation of architects, politicians, and public health officials expanded to include the expertise of economists, sociologists, geographers, and lawyers, as the intricacies of city planning became better understood. Yet urban planning is not only of concern to city planners and academics. As Lévi-Strauss suggests, the shape of the urban environment is something to which we all contribute every day, as we make choices regarding where we will live and what type of transportation we will use. Furthermore, although decisions are made at the federal, state, and local levels without the approval of the general public, their effects are felt far beyond the circle of those involved in the planning process.

Anyone who has played the computer game SimCity will be familiar with the general features of urban planning. It can be described as the attempt to organize and design urban places—from major cities and suburbs to small towns and rural villages—with the aim of meeting certain goals, such as improving efficiency and quality of life. It incorporates all the various aspects that are a part of urban life, such as transportation, housing, the economy, architecture, public facilities, the environment, open spaces, zoning laws, land-use regulations, community development, and resource conservation. Moreover, the process of urban planning involves the complex interplay of numerous parties: the federal government, for example, allocates tax revenues to support the development of transportation infrastructure and public housing; governors and state legislators produce statewide land-use planning regulations; city officials design downtown beautification plans; business groups lobby for zoning changes and tax incentives; real estate developers and architects build homes, offices, and cultural centers; and citizens join organizations and attend city council meetings to voice their concerns.

The articles collected here present a sampling of current developments in urban planning. The book is divided into five sections highlighting key aspects, beginning with a general introduction to population growth and urban sprawl and progressing to more specific treatments of various types of urban development. Issues in the field are rarely encountered in isolation, and readers will detect a fair amount of overlap. While a volume of this size clearly cannot cover the subject in its entirety, it is hoped that the articles will provide an introduction to topics of substantial interest to the general reader, stimulating further research. The last decade has seen the emergence of several new trends in urban planning whose implications are only now becoming clear.

The first section of this book examines the topic of urban sprawl, the ubiquitous spread of low-density urbanization across the American landscape. The 2000 census shows that the U.S. population grew by 32 million people between 1990 and 2000, and it is expected to gain 120 million by 2050, for a total population exceeding 400 million. While some of this growth has been absorbed by cities, the majority has gone to the suburbs, where it is evident in the continual development occurring along the urban fringe. The article by Haya El Nasser and Paul Overberg introduces the concept of sprawl in light of a recent study by *USA Today*. Then, Don Finley examines the argument that the outward spread of urban communities, made possible by America's automobile-oriented culture, may be linked to an increase in obesity and pedestrian injuries. Olga Bonfiglio's article discusses the economic and racial effects that sprawl has had on cities, and Dennis Hevesi examines the history of sprawl in the U.S. and explains that "smart growth"—an approach to planning that calls for walkable communities and improved mass transit—is being widely touted as the key to remedying sprawl's negative effects.

Section II showcases various contemporary trends in urban development, beginning with the nostalgic, traditional design of New Urbanism, also known as neo-traditionalism. The opening article, by New Urbanist doyens Andres Duany and Elizabeth Plater-Zyberk, presents the principles of the movement along with criticisms of the urban environment produced by sprawl. This is followed by Deborah K. Dietsch's article examining current applications of New Urbanist ideas, plus a negative assessment offered by Peter Gordon in an interview with Rick Henderson and Adrian T. Moore. Next, Jay Walljasper looks at how smart-growth measures are being enacted in Portland, Oregon, and Jonathan Walters sheds light on the issues at stake when large retailers like Target and Wal-Mart seek to build their superstores on the outskirts of small towns. Jonathan Barnett writes about current changes taking place in edge cities. The last article, by Nicole White, describes how a struggling Miami neighborhood is seeking to court development by offering tax incentives to new businesses.

The third section focuses on transportation issues. Although the term "transportation infrastructure" includes roads, public transportation systems, airports, water transport, and railroads, the articles in this section focus on questions pertaining to automobile traffic and mass transit, as these issues have been at the center of popular debate in recent years. Roads and highways are vital to the nation's economy, serving as the primary means of moving people and goods from one place to another, yet as Joan Lowy explains in the section's first article, traffic congestion is growing at a faster rate than roads are being built to ease it. Popular methods of combating traffic, such as congestion pricing and smart-growth initiatives, are addressed by Martin Wachs, who concludes that information technology offers a potent alternative. Jane Holtz Kay writes that light-rail transit systems are gaining popularity, even in sprawling southwestern cities such as Phoenix and Dallas. Finally, Robert Campbell presents an account of the Big Dig, a massive project to demolish Boston's severely congested central thoroughfare and rebuild it underground.

The next section looks at current approaches to addressing the nation's housing needs. Olivera Perkins discusses the changes taking place in federally subsidized public housing in Cleveland, Ohio, part of a national trend to replace blighted apartment complexes with low-rise buildings and garden apartments. Ron Scherer's article looks at the emphasis on mixed-income policies in public housing, while Chris Palladino writes about a neighborhood redevelopment plan designed to create opportunities for home ownership for low-income families. Concluding the section is an article by James B. Goodno discussing the use of trust funds to create affordable housing.

The fifth and final section takes a broader look at what is being done to make our cities vital, healthy, and interesting places to live at the turn of the millennium. Nicolai Ouroussoff leads off with an article suggesting that American architecture could benefit from an influx of idealism. Cathleen McGuigan and David Jefferson write about the revitalization efforts being made in downtown Los Angeles. Gillian Flaccus takes a look at "ecoroofs" in Portland, Oregon, and Janet Frankston reports on an experimental brownfield redevelopment and transportation project underway at Atlantic Station in Atlanta, Georgia. Alan Erhenhalt discusses Metropolis 2020, a regional governing plan proposed by Chicago's business community. Finally, Casey Nelson Blake outlines a vision for the future of "ground zero," the former site of the World Trade Center, which was destroyed in the terrorist attacks of September 11, 2001.

I would like to thank all the authors and publishers who granted permission for their work to appear in this volume. I am especially grateful to all those who assisted in the production of the book, including Lynn Messina, Sandra Watson, Jennifer Peloso, Gray Young, Rich Stein, Norris Smith, and Clifford Thompson. Many thanks as well to Shaina Feinberg and Jessica Karaska for their helpful advice during the research of this project.

Andrew I. Cavin
August 2003

I. Urban Sprawl

Editor's Introduction

Urban sprawl—the rapid expansion of urban development across the American landscape—has surfaced as a popular topic of debate in recent years. According to a recent study by the non-profit Pew Center for Civic Journalism, cited by Haya El Nasser and Paul Overberg in the first article of this chapter, when voters were asked to name the most important problem in their communities, sprawl and traffic tied for first with crime and violence; issues such as education, health, and medicine came afterwards. In 1999 Vice President Al Gore introduced a multi-billion-dollar "liveability agenda" with measures designed to limit sprawl, propelling the term into national discussion, and for a time he made the issue a part of his 2000 presidential election campaign.

Sprawl is not a new phenomenon. Its roots are generally traced back to the 1950s, when America experienced the first large-scale planned movement of people out of cities and into outlying areas. This period saw the birth of the suburbs as the residential ideal. The end of World War II was followed by an economic boom and unprecedented population growth. The return of about 16 million GIs after the war and an escalation of marriage and birth rates meant a sudden increase in the need for housing. The government met the demand with special funding measures: the Federal Housing Administration (FHA) offered low-payment, low-interest loans to encourage home buyers, and the Veterans Administration (VA) offered GIs excellent mortgage rates. Real-estate developers followed suit by building mass-produced neighborhoods outside of cities, consisting of row upon row of identical, inexpensive, box-like houses. The most famous of these was Levittown, Long Island, a suburb east of New York City, the first of many Levittowns built by William Levitt. In 1956 Congress passed the Interstate Highway Act, providing $26 billion to construct 41,000 miles of interstate roads for the new suburbanites to commute to and from work. Thus the stage was set for the decades of urban expansion that followed.

Sprawl has dominated headlines about urban growth in recent years, but, for a term in such wide use, its definition is far from precise. For environmentalists concerned about the loss of land and the damage to ecosystems, sprawl simply means growth. Others tend to associate it with a particular kind of growth, such as the endless suburban landscape of Los Angeles, or the proliferation of drab strip malls and office parks that line the nation's highways. In "What You Don't Know About Sprawl," El Nasser and Overberg discuss the findings of a nationwide study on sprawl by *USA Today* that attempts to clarify the issue. Using population density rather than size as a measure, the study was able to rank the country's 271 metropolitan areas according to their degree of sprawl, producing some unexpected results. Los Angeles, considered by many to be the archetype of sprawl, actually ranked fairly low on the scale, whereas Portland, Oregon, usually considered an exemplar of managed growth, ranked higher. (For U.S. Census Bureau maps showing urban population by state and the percent change in total population from 1990 to 2000 by stte, see Appendixes A and B on pages 169 and 170.)

Don Finley, in "Poor Urban Planning Hinders the Pedestrian," discusses recent arguments that sprawling metro areas, designed around the automobile and not the pedestrian, may be linked to health factors such as obesity and to higher numbers of pedestrian injuries. Finley discusses the history of car-oriented communities that began with Levittown, pointing out that those early communities were actually pedestrian-friendly, featuring homes, parks, and shopping areas within walking distance of one another. Changes in zoning laws over time, however, have resulted in fractured communities with residential subdivisions in one area and large commercial centers in another, causing increased car-dependency.

Urban sprawl has also been linked to economic and racial inequality. While some major cities—Chicago, Atlanta, Denver, and Boston, for example—continued to grow during the 1990s, others have not been able to recover from decades of urban sprawl that have drained city centers of their former middle-class inhabitants. In "Addressing Urban Sprawl," Olga Bonfiglio highlights the deleterious effect that suburban flight has had on Detroit, Michigan, where, as in other cities, middle-class whites were able to move to the suburbs in search of better schools and safer streets, leaving behind poorer residents, usually minority and immigrant populations, forced to cope with run-down neighborhoods, abandoned buildings, and failing schools. As people left, so did the jobs. Bonfiglio reports on the recent attempt of the Catholic Archdiocese of Detroit to launch an initiative to improve mass transit in an effort to reinvigorate the inner city by linking it with jobs in the suburbs.

The movements towards improving public transportation and building walkable communities, as outlined in the preceding articles, are just two of several prominent means of countering the effects of urban sprawl. Dennis Hevesi, in "Antidotes to Sprawl Taking Many Forms," groups these and several others—including an emphasis on compact building design, mixed-use development, the preservation of open space, and development directed towards existing communities—under the umbrella term of "smart growth," a buzzword for the way urban planners and developers are reacting to increased public concern over the sprawling urban environment. In addition to introducing smart growth and briefly touching on the history of sprawl, Hevesi discusses recent projects where abandoned developments, such as old malls, industrial sites, and deteriorated waterfonts, are being redeveloped to include places for people to live, work, shop, and walk—creating what is known as "mixed-use" development. The topic of smart growth is taken up again in the following chapter in articles treating one of its most visible and controversial manifestations, the New Urbanist movement.

What You Don't Know About Sprawl[1]

By Haya El Nasser and Paul Overberg
USA Today, February 22, 2001

Los Angeles, whose legendary traffic congestion and spread-out development have epitomized suburban sprawl for decades, isn't so sprawling after all.

In fact, Portland, Ore., the metropolitan area that enacted the nation's toughest anti-growth laws, sprawls more.

Worse than either of them is Nashville, which is the nation's most sprawling metro of 1 million people or more.

Those are some of the findings of a *USA Today* analysis of population trends over the past decade in the nation's 271 metro areas.

Across the country, people are debating the issue of sprawl as governments try to reconcile growing needs for new housing and commercial development with demands to protect open space. This newspaper's study shows why: 83% of metro areas are more sprawling now than in 1990.

To quantify sprawl, *USA Today* developed an index that analyzes how densely developed a metro is today and how that changed during the '90s. The result is the *USA Today* Sprawl Index.

Some findings from the analysis defy conventional wisdom:

- A boom in population doesn't necessarily trigger sprawl. It can occur when the population in a metropolitan area is shrinking.

- A number of small metropolitan areas (pop. 250,000 or fewer) in some of the more pastoral corners of the country sprawl more than large metro areas. In fact, most of the nation's major metro areas (pop. 1 million or more) are experiencing the least sprawl.

Other key findings:

- The availability of water is a major factor in limiting or allowing sprawl. For example, in a booming desert city such as Las Vegas, the scarcity of water forces development to stay close to the city's edge—and its municipal water lines—and not leap-frog open space.

- Geography is another major factor limiting or allowing sprawl. Oceans, mountains and other natural barriers can force a metro to grow compactly while flat land can allow development of any kind.

The ocean and mountains encircling Los Angeles are powerful anti-sprawl forces today. This once-sprawling city is running out of room and turning inward to grow. But in the Southeast, few natural barriers limit growth. Unrelenting sprawl along Interstates 85 and 20 is creating a "string city" that stretches 600 miles between Raleigh, N.C., and Birmingham, Ala.

The forces of water and geography are evident in the sprawl index. Of the 17 major metropolitan areas that sprawl the most, 16 are east of the Mississippi. Four of the top five are in the Southeast: Nashville; Charlotte; Greensboro, N.C.; and Atlanta.

- Local and state governments' efforts to restrict sprawl are growing but have had limited impact.

- A lack of regional government planning can foster sprawl. In metros in the Northeast and Midwest, dozens of local governments regulate development. The result is fragmented planning.

How the Index Works

The *USA Today* Sprawl Index is based on a simple measure of sprawl: population density. Each metro area's index score is based on two density measurements:

- Population density today. Density is the percentage of a metro area's population that lives in "urbanized areas." The Census Bureau defines urbanized areas as those parts of a metro with 1,000 or more residents per square mile.

- Change in population density during the 1990s. The second component of the index measures how much a metro's percentage in urbanized areas increased or decreased from 1990 to 1999.

The metropolitan areas were ranked 1 through 271 on each measurement (lower numbers represent less sprawl). The two rankings were added to produce each metro area's sprawl index score. The highest possible score is 542, the lowest is 2.

For example, in the Louisville metro area, 76% of the population lived in urbanized areas in 1999. That gave Louisville a rank of 85 among the 271 metros. In 1990, 79.6% lived in urbanized areas. Louisville's 4.5% drop during the '90s gave it a rank of 221. Adding those two rankings of 85 and 221 produced a sprawl index score of 306. Of the 271 metros, 108 have higher numbers than Louisville, which means they sprawl more, and 162 have lower numbers and sprawl less.

More Space than Necessary?

Because sprawl occurs in different ways and at different rates across the country, it's difficult for people and governments to agree on how to deal with it.

When the non-profit Pew Center for Civic Journalism asked voters to name the most important problem in their communities, sprawl and traffic tied for first with crime and violence. Each was cited by 18% of those surveyed. Issues such as education and health and medicine trailed far behind in the poll.

Across the country, the desire for new, affordable housing and commercial space creates sprawl.

Experts say that finding a common definition of whether a metro area is sprawling—or not—is a necessary first step toward helping people understand how to deal with it. *Webster's New World College Dictionary* defines sprawl as spreading out in an awkward way "so as to take up more space than is necessary." As with most discussions involving sprawl, though, the meaning of "more space than is necessary" is debatable.

Robert Lang, director of urban and metropolitan research at the Fannie Mae Foundation, says, "There's a big public policy imperative to do something about what people call sprawl. It would be nice to have a definition."

By using population density to measure sprawl, the *USA Today* index is able to rank all 271 metropolitan areas based on their degree of sprawl today. And comparing population density in 1990 and 1999 shows how these metro areas are growing. Armed with that knowledge, government officials, developers and residents can debate what measures—if any—they should take.

A Love-Hate Relationship

Across the country, the desire for new, affordable housing and commercial space creates sprawl. Cheap land outside urbanized areas allows people to buy their own homes. It also provides an escape for people who perceive only downsides to life in the city—from crime and low-quality public education to high housing costs.

At the same time, people want more parks and wildlife preserves. They want more green space, farms and unbroken natural scenery. And as development pushes ever farther from the urbanized areas of many metros, residents are becoming increasingly fed up with traffic jams and strip malls that result. Many are calling on the government to stop the sprawl that their very move to the suburbs helped create.

Since 1997, 22 states have enacted some type of land-use law designed to rein in sprawl. In 1999 alone, lawmakers introduced 1,000 bills in state legislatures, and they passed more than 200. In 2000, there were 553 growth measures on the ballot in 38 states, according to a report to be released Monday by the Brookings Institution's Center on Urban and Metropolitan Policy. Voters approved more than 70% of them. In fast-growing counties, people are elect-ing "smart-growth" candidates to public office who advocate restrict-ing sprawl.

Americans are even willing to spend their money to protect green space. In the summer of 1999, eight homeowners in Warren Town-ship, N.J., spent $125,000 to buy seven acres near their homes to keep the land wooded. Around the same time, about 400 families in the affluent Cleveland suburbs of Chagrin Falls and Bentleyville contributed $300,000 to preserve 62 acres.

The debate over how to control sprawl often pits the public good against self-interest. Most people agree that protecting natural resources and open space is important, but few are willing to give up the right to do what they want with their own land.

Some free-market thinkers say the sprawl debate is much ado about nothing. The country has plenty of space, says Sam Staley, director of the Urban Futures Program for Reason Public Policy Institute in Los Angeles. The 80% of Americans who live in metro areas should have the right to choose between a condo in the city and a home on a big lot in the suburbs.

As communities debate what to do about it, they can't agree on what sprawl is, or even whether it's good or bad.

"Quality of life. It starts with that," Staley says. "Then the question becomes, 'Does sprawl compromise quality of life?' I don't think it does because people are choosing to move to these communities all the time. There are alternatives to sprawl in every major city in the United States, but people are choosing not to return to those neighborhoods."

As a result, sprawl remains a national dilemma. People are fed up with it, yet they like what it provides. And they don't like the alternative to sprawl: living in a more crowded urban environment.

As communities debate what to do about it, they can't agree on what sprawl is, or even whether it's good or bad. Sprawl is blamed for social isolation and obesity (people driving everywhere), asthma and global warming (auto emissions), flooding and erosion (too much pavement), the demise of small farms (devel-opers buying their land) and the extinction of wildlife (natural areas being overrun by development). At the same time, it is credited with creating safe neighborhoods, affordable housing and good schools. In short, a chance to live the American dream.

Natural Barriers

A key finding of the sprawl index is the impact of geography and water. Mountains and other natural barriers and limited supplies of water have prevented many Western cities from sprawling; flat land and plentiful water have allowed most Eastern cities to grow as they please. As a result, most Western metro areas have fairly low sprawl index scores and many Eastern cities have high scores.

In the West, a metro area's water often comes from one source. New growth tends to occur right at the edge of existing development so that it can tap into the municipal water supply. In the East, a developer can put a subdivision miles beyond the end of a municipal water line and drill wells and install septic tanks. This ability to leapfrog open spaces leads to sprawl. Mountains, oceans and other natural barriers also prevent development from spreading. Once a metro area butts up against them, its population can increase only if development becomes denser. Single-family lots become smaller, and condominium and apartment buildings go up.

The Los Angeles metro area has a population of 16 million and seems sprawling to many. But if the Atlanta metro (pop. 3.8 million) had as many people as Los Angeles and the same population density Atlanta has, it would occupy many more square miles than Los Angeles.

That point is reflected in the sprawl index scores for the two metro areas. Los Angeles has a score of 78, which is even lower than metropolitan New York's (82), which is known for its sky-scraper-studded downtown. Atlanta has a sprawl index score of 392.

In the Atlanta metropolitan area, 72.9% lived in urbanized areas in 1990, and by 1999, that figure had dropped to 67.4%. Throughout the '90s, Atlanta continued to sprawl as people moving to Atlanta chose less-populated parts of the metro area. In Los Angeles, 94.9% lived in urbanized areas in 1990. By 1999, that percentage had dropped only slightly, to 94.3%.

In the West, growth occurs in an orderly fashion because it's tethered to those water lines.

In the East, especially the Southeast, growth can be disorderly. Developers can buy cheap rural land and build on it because they don't have to worry about public water and sewer facilities. This leapfrog development consumes vast amounts of land and traps green space—pastures, cropland and woods—between developments. A population that occupies 1,000 square miles in a metro area constrained by natural forces could occupy several times that in one without constraints.

This untamed ability to sprawl has produced rapidly merging metropolitan areas along I-85 and I-20 between Raleigh, N.C. (index score: 271), and Birmingham, Ala. (323). Development there has unfurled from big urban centers such as Charlotte, N.C., and Atlanta to the rural towns in between.

Call them "countrified cities," Lang says. "It's easy when you just develop across a series of off-ramps to never develop any cohesion."

The sprawl index list of big metro areas (pop. 1 million or more) shows how the availability of land and water has affected growth in the Southeast. Nashville (index score: 478) is No. 1 on the list. Charlotte (454); Greensboro, N.C. (437); and Atlanta (392) are in the top five. Four others are in the top 15: Memphis (329); Orlando (290); Raleigh (271); and Washington (261).

Miami-Fort Lauderdale (69) is a big metropolitan in the region that is not high on the sprawl index. Miami shares the fate of cities in the West. Geography pins it into a 25-mile-wide area between the Atlantic Ocean and the Everglades. It ranks on the sprawl index right above San Diego (66), which is confined to 30 miles between ocean and mountains.

The availability of cheap land in the Southeast and the Midwest also has turned many small metros (pop. 250,000 or fewer) into major engines of sprawl. These communities appeal to companies and individuals that want cheap land and want to escape the congestion of big metros. They're also close to major urban centers—and their jobs, services and entertainment. Examples include Janesville, Wis. (263), west of Milwaukee, and St. Cloud, Minn. (231), which is just outside Minneapolis.

Man-made Restrictions

The effect of government on sprawl—and its limitations—can be seen best in metropolitan Portland, Ore. For years, Portland has fought to prevent the sprawl it saw shape Los Angeles. In 1973, Portland established an urban growth boundary to stop development and preserve open space beyond a certain line. The boundary encouraged denser development inside it.

However, Portland's sprawl index score of 221 puts it roughly in the middle of the list of big metros. One reason: Growth is escaping the control of the Portland Metropolitan Council, a regional board of three counties and 24 cities that set up the boundary. Developers are jumping over land that is under the council's jurisdiction and building on land beyond it. Growth is occurring to the south in Salem, Ore., and to the north across the state line in Vancouver, Wash. Both cities are part of the Portland metropolitan area, as defined by the Census Bureau, and are within easy commuting distance of Portland.

Las Vegas (159) is an example of the impact of both natural and man-made barriers. The nation's gambling capital is gaining people at a faster pace than Atlanta. Unlike Atlanta, Las Vegas is not sprawling across miles and miles of open land. That's because the metro area is in a desert and has limited water. It's also hemmed in by mountains and vast amounts of federally owned land, including Nellis Air Force Base and Lake Mead National Recreation Area.

"Las Vegas has an urban growth boundary. It's called federal land," says Bill Fulton of Solimar Research Group, an urban research and planning firm in Ventura, Calif.

Las Vegas' population has grown 60% in the past decade to 1.4 million, but more than three-quarters of those new residents moved into urbanized areas. Las Vegas has experienced orderly growth. New development has occurred at the edge of old, rather than leapfrogging open space, as in Atlanta.

Powerful Cultural Forces

Racial tensions and urban decay fueled much of the flight to the suburbs in metro areas in the Midwest and Northeast. Today, those metro areas rank high on the *USA Today* Sprawl Index. On the list of big metros, Grand Rapids, Mich. (357); Indianapolis (299); and Cincinnati (292) rank among the top 15. They're all highly segregated areas, according to several studies of Census data from 1990.

"By many measures, the Midwest has both the highest racial segregation and the most-concentrated poverty at the cores," says George Galster, an urban planning professor at Wayne State University in Detroit. "That centrifugal push makes it possible for developers to offer ever more distant alternatives to 'urban problems.'"

Local politics also contributes to sprawl in these regions. In the Northeast, metros are made up of many municipalities, which makes it harder to develop a regional growth plan. The same is true in the Midwest, a region settled by Northeasterners who brought with them a tradition of town meetings and local control. Metropolitan Detroit has 280 local governments; metro New York more than 560.

"Each of them can adopt their separate zoning and housing and land-use codes," Galster says.

These disparate interests work against regional planning. One municipality can restrict growth, but if a neighboring town welcomes it, sprawl continues.

Sprawl Can Be Deceiving

Often, the debate over sprawl and what to do—if anything—to control it comes down to perception. In Charlotte, trees dominate the land outside the tight downtown skyline. But the forest is just an illusion because development is hidden beneath the foliage.

That's true of many places on the East Coast, where flat land and dense trees mask sprawl. Lang points to metropolitan Boston (205), which ranks with Minneapolis (203) and Detroit (208) as average among big metros on the sprawl index. "People say, 'Boston is the densest place I know,' but you don't see the two-acre and three-acre lots out in the suburbs because of the trees," he says. "In Los Angeles, they see everything because there are no trees."

Of course there are trees, but in a semiarid climate like Southern California's, vegetation is not as naturally lush. In the West, any development on treeless hillsides is in plain view.

Many Western cities also appear sprawling because of the way they are designed. Los Angeles has single-family homes stretching for miles. Away from downtown, few high-rises break up the monotony.

"For some people, that's sprawl," says Rolf Pendall, an urban planning professor at Cornell University in Ithaca, N.Y.

However, population density is the key determinant of sprawl. Those single-family homes in Los Angeles are on very small lots. In the East, older metros appear to sprawl less because their packed, 19th-century cores and tall buildings form an image of density. But sprawl still exists. It's just occurring miles from downtown.

> *Individual choices and lifestyles ultimately shape development in this country.*

"Sprawl is so multifaceted and takes on so many different forms across the country that it's probably going to require different solutions," Lang says.

Struggle for Solutions

Everyone is pushing for "smart" growth, but no one can agree on what "dumb" growth is.

Some planners call for more roads as a way to ease traffic congestion. Others say building or widening roads creates a bigger traffic mess and encourages more development. Some advocate single-family houses on big lots. Others insist the solution is more apartments and small homes to accommodate more people on less land.

Some say housing should be built close to mass transit and within walking distance of stores, schools and other services to get cars off the road. Others argue that Americans don't want to live in a more crowded urban setting or give up their cars. Some want strict growth boundaries. Others say that limiting development pushes up housing prices and reduces the stock of affordable housing.

They agree on one thing, though: Municipalities must plan better.

Faced with mounting pressure from residents, environmentalists and other interest groups and local officials, eight states have approved comprehensive growth-management plans that require local governments to prevent development where roads and sewers don't exist. In 1998, Tennessee required municipalities to set up urban-growth boundaries. In 1999, Georgia set up a regional transportation authority that has veto power over major construction in a 13-county area in and around Atlanta.

But most other states that have been dragged into a problem that's usually left to local government are sticking to laws that get little resistance. They're setting aside funds to buy open space, farmland or forests. Some are creating tax incentives for landowners to donate development rights to the state or conservationists.

Even as planners and elected officials grapple with sprawl, individual choices and lifestyles ultimately shape development in this country.

Latanya Wells, 37, grew up in inner-city Detroit and never thought of leaving. "It was clean. You felt safe. People were neighborly," she says. Over the years, her neighborhood changed for the worse. By the time she finally left in 1997, "you barely knew your neighbors or spoke to your neighbors. There were bars on the windows."

Wells, her sister and brother—all teachers in Detroit public schools—did what millions of Americans have done for decades: They moved to the suburbs. They briefly considered, but rejected, housing going up in some of the most distressed neighborhoods downtown, part of the city's effort to bring people back to the city. "We looked around the neighborhood and thought: We're going to be scared to go to our cars," she says. "It's still rough down there."

They chose Southfield, 13 miles from their jobs in the city. An older suburb packed with strip malls and lookalike homes, Southfield is a sprawling eyesore to some. But not to Wells.

"It's a matter of perception," she says. "I like it."

Poor Urban Planning Hinders the Pedestrian[2]

By Don Finley
San Antonio Express-News, December 10, 2002

Sylvia Kelepis is dashing across a downtown street, a step or two behind her friend Penny the poodle. Both are wrapped in sweaters to ward off the early morning chill on their daily stroll.

Kelepis, 69, retired here from New York City—a place where crossing the street might be considered a contact sport.

But New York has nothing on her retirement home. Two years ago, a report named Tampa-St. Petersburg the most dangerous urban area in the nation for pedestrians. It recently was bumped to No. 2 by Orlando.

Kelepis isn't certain why her city might be so dangerous. Maybe it's because everyone here seems to be from somewhere else. Maybe all those regional driving styles make for a deadly combination.

"People drive the way they're accustomed to driving in the places where they used to live," she said.

Experts have a different explanation. Like much of the southern United States that experienced explosive growth after World War II, large parts of Tampa and St. Petersburg were built for cars, not people.

And now, faced with an epidemic of obesity, a growing coalition of health and policy officials, planners and advocates is looking at ways to reintroduce Americans to the lost art of walking down the street.

"I believe declines in physical activity reflect changes in the neighborhoods in which we live," said Dr. William Dietz, director of nutrition and physical activity at the Centers for Disease Control and Prevention in Atlanta.

People in older cities such as New York and Philadelphia are able to walk or ride a bike for everyday activity, Dietz said. Those cities are characterized by "a very dense pattern of housing, with lots of street connections [to] centralized schools and shopping facilities."

"Contrast that with Atlanta and the suburbs of San Antonio and other cities along the South and Southwest, where we see neighborhood patterns with cul-de-sacs, often no sidewalks. Schools and shopping centers are located quite some distance [away], and the only alternative is to get in a car and drive to do these errands," Dietz said.

Michelle Ernst, a senior analyst with the Surface Transportation Policy Project and co-author of the report, said: "What we found was that the worst areas in the U.S. [for pedestrians] tended to be cities in the South or the West. And nearly all the cities are in newer, sprawling metro areas."

Americans are walking less—about 42 percent less than they did 20 years ago, according to the Nationwide Personal Transportation Survey. During that time, the amount of obesity has grown by about the same percentage.

> *Those who do walk are taking their lives in their hands.*

Nearly one in four trips Americans make are one mile or less, yet three quarters of those short trips are made by car.

Those who do walk, say critics such as Ernst, are taking their lives in their hands.

Chris Hagelin, who studies transportation issues at the University of South Florida, says Tampa-St. Pete suffers from "stereotypical sprawl development, where you have multilane roads separating residential and commercial areas."

"I know that the majority of the pedestrian injuries and fatalities in Florida are midblock crossings," Hagelin said. "That's because we've developed these huge, multilane roads where the intersections are a half-mile apart. How many people are going to walk half a mile, cross the street, and walk back half a mile—just to cross the street?"

How much of the obesity problem is a result of poor urban planning? The beginning of an answer might be found on the opposite coast.

San Diego, Calif.

The sign on Adams Avenue welcomes visitors to Normal Heights, but there's nothing much normal about it anymore. Normal Heights is the kind of traditional neighborhood that steadily has become endangered in America.

People walk here. The supermarket, the dry cleaners, restaurants and bookstores are within walking distance to houses and apartments. It has a kind of old neighborhood feel, with storefronts close to the street.

"There are weeks when I don't even leave the neighborhood," said Mike Magers, who walks most days from home to Smitty's Service, the garage his grandfather started here in 1945.

"Of course, they're pretty dull weeks," he adds with a laugh. "Those are weeks when I'm mowing the lawn, picking up dog poop and paying the bills."

Elsewhere in California, there are a few communities that are pedestrian friendly—and if you happen to be a millionaire, you might be able to afford to live there. Carmel is an example. So is Palo Alto.

But Normal Heights isn't wealthy. In fact, probably the only reason it retained its character over the years is because it had deteriorated to the point that nobody wanted to spend money paving it over.

"I remember the first night I lived here," Magers said. "I bought my house from a little old lady. I think most of us who bought houses did. She was securing her house by taking a wedge and pushing it under the door so no one could get in. That was how she locked her doors. I remember how scared I was, because the [police] helicopters were flying over every night."

That has changed. Residents banded together and worked with police to make the neighborhood safer. And, realizing the unique flavor of their community, they formed a neighborhood association to keep it that way.

And now, housing prices have skyrocketed (at last reaching the

---

"You can kind of think of the obesity epidemic as the canary in the coal mine. It's an indicator that things are going really bad with our society."—Dr. James Sallis, professor of psychology

---

insane altitude of the rest of the California housing market). Lots of people, it seems, want to move to Normal Heights.

Dr. James Sallis, a professor of psychology at San Diego State University, was curious about Normal Heights, too. Sallis is interested in how neighborhoods encourage or hinder physical activity.

He recruited 50 volunteers from Normal Heights and 50 others from a more typical suburban neighborhood in San Diego. He gave each volunteer a device to wear that measured physical movement. His study found people in Normal Heights chalked up 30 minutes more physical activity a week than their crosstown counterparts.

"You can say 30 minutes a week is not that much, but this is 30 minutes a week, every week, forever," Sallis said.

The Normal Heights study is being expanded on a much larger scale in Atlanta. And Sallis is part of a new Robert Wood Johnson Foundation effort to study communities and how people walk in them.

"You can kind of think of the obesity epidemic as the canary in the coal mine," Sallis said. "It's an indicator that things are going really bad with our society.

"We've been building cities differently since World War II than they've ever been built before, based on the assumption that we're going to drive everywhere we go. So now we're in a situation where we do that, and we don't think that it's really working out that well."

Long Island, N.Y.

How did that happen? In the years after World War II, a lot of people were drawn to suburbs. Cities were crowded, deteriorating, dirty. Cars made it easy to commute from subdivisions carved out of farmland, where big back yards and driveways were possible.

"We were paying $75 a month for rent" in Coney Island, Stanley Rosenzweig recalled. "And what happened was, they started tearing down the older houses. We got inundated with cockroaches and mice. We packed up all our stuff and put it in boxes, and before we moved in, we opened up every box outside to make sure we weren't going to bring cockroaches in this house."

Rosenzweig and his wife, Francine, moved 35 miles away to Levittown, a pleasant-enough, tree-shaded neighborhood with winding streets and little houses built over a 1,500-acre potato field in Nas-

---

"We've been building cities . . . based on the assumption that we're going to drive everywhere we go."—**Dr. James Sallis**

---

sau County, considered by urban historians to be the first modern suburb built for cars.

Levittown opened March 7, 1949, to instant success. World War II was over, and millions of couples were looking to start new lives. Anticipating the pent-up demand—fueled by cheap new government-sponsored home loans—Bill Levitt introduced mass production techniques to the construction of single-family homes.

More than 1,000 couples lined up the first day to spend $6,990 for a tiny (by today's standards) Cape Cod-style house, each with a 12-by-16 foot living room, radiant heating in the floor, and built-in refrigerator, stove and Admiral television set.

A car was a necessity. Jobs were in the city. The train station was, and is, a couple of miles away.

Still, given the controversy that surrounds all the suburbs that followed, Levittown is surprisingly walkable. It had to be.

In those days, "the husband took the car and the woman was home," said Ann Glorioso, a reference librarian at Levittown Public Library, and an unofficial historian of the neighborhood.

Levitt "designed village greens into the design of Levittown," Glorioso said. "Those village greens had drug stores and little grocery stores. There are six village greens in Levittown. So that no matter where you lived, you could walk to that green and do your shopping—at least a good part of it."

No longer. The parks and sidewalks are still there, but not the stores. Like in every other neighborhood in America, most families here have two cars and two careers. The evolution of retail has meant an end to the small, neighborhood store—including those in Levittown.

"When we lived in Coney Island you didn't need really a car," Rosenzweig said. "You had the trains and the subways. Out here you need a car because you're so far away from everything."

San Antonio

Gordon Hartman built his first house at age 19, right after high school. He sold it, and the following year he built two more.

"I thought, this is kind of cool," he recalled, smiling. "Now, we start 1½ houses every day."

"During the '90s, if you didn't gate something, you were almost committing suicide with your development."—Gordon Hartman, **home-building business owner**

Born and reared here, the son of a former TV weatherman and city councilman, Hartman owns the biggest locally owned home-building business in San Antonio.

He's taken some well-publicized risks, building in inner-city neighborhoods where few would go. But largely, he's been adept at staying ahead of market trends. He's had to. It's difficult for a local firm to compete with the big national builders that dominate the market.

The first priority for his customers—a good percentage of whom are single women, for some reason—is living near a good school. The ability to walk to those schools is not such a big issue.

Fear may be a reason. Hartman estimates San Antonio has more homes in gated communities per capita than any other American city. If neighborhoods with long, winding streets that only connect to other streets at one end make walking to schools or stores difficult, putting a wall around those neighborhoods makes it almost impossible.

"We have a perception that if we gate our subdivisions, we are more secure," Hartman said. "As a developer-builder here, we have recently tried to back away from that. But I will tell you that during the '90s, if you didn't gate something, you were almost committing suicide with your development."

Now San Antonio, like many other cities, is starting to rethink how its neighborhoods are laid out. The recently passed Unified Development Code requires better sidewalks, more "connectivity" among (or ways in and out of) neighborhoods, some zoning changes and incentives for neighborhood parks.

"We don't really build neighborhoods anymore," said Doug Lipscomb, an architect with Ford, Powell and Carson. "We build housing subdivisions over here. Commercial centers with big-box retail over there. Those things aren't thought about in an integrated way."

Advocates of more traditional neighborhoods place much of the blame for today's mess on zoning, which a century ago began separating dirty and dangerous industry from the places people lived. No one, for instance, wanted to live next door to a tannery.

In the years that followed, city planners promoted the idea of separating all city functions. With new construction largely halted through the Depression and World War II, that idea wasn't put into practice until the 1950s—when millions began abandoning New York, Chicago and Detroit for fast-growing cities such as Phoenix, Los Angeles and San Antonio.

San Antonio's 1938 building codes allowed neighborhoods with both homes and stores, Lipscomb noted. By 1965, those codes had been rewritten, and everything had to be separate.

Now, many want to reassemble the puzzle pieces that make up American cities. And while that sounds impossible, some urban planners believe cities are rebuilt every 60 years. The hard part, they say, is deciding what kind of cities we want.

Not everyone is convinced that rethinking cities will affect obesity.

"The whole effort to extend these sorts of development issues with [obesity and other health problems] is dishonest and dangerous," said Ronald Utt, who has written about sprawl for the Heritage Foundation, a think tank that promotes conservative public policies.

To tackle the obesity epidemic, Utt said, Americans should focus on the junk they eat, rather than how cities and transportation influence physical activity.

"To the extent that we focus on the real reasons," he said, "we induce the changes that we want—not by using this as an agenda item to advance some particular cause."

For Hartman, the question is more a practical one.

"When I was growing up I used to go to Winn's. I could ride my bike or walk. Now I go to Target or I go to Wal-Mart. And when you have a Wal-Mart, you only have one every five miles.

"So even with the UDC, we're not going to make all of these major adjustments. Because the economics will not allow us to have the little corner guy who just sells the milk, and the guy who just sells a few nails. Those days are over."

Addressing Urban Sprawl[3]

By Olga Bonfiglio
America, November 4, 2002

When leaders of the archdiocese of Detroit began looking for solutions to the mounting poverty in the Detroit metropolitan area, they discovered that the traditional ministries of soup kitchens, clothing drives and holiday baskets were not changing the impoverished environment of the city. The city's decline was more structural, institutional and political, and they realized that they were looking squarely into an injustice that had developed and permeated the community for the past 40 years—urban sprawl. The archdiocese, which serves 1.5 million Catholics in six counties of southeastern Michigan, joined a coalition of interfaith religious congregations that is working hard not only to curb and contain urban sprawl, but also to approach it as a moral issue that demands a response of justice and equality for all people living in the region.

Urban sprawl is a consequence of federal, state and local land-use policies that have resulted in an epidemic of unplanned growth, the voracious consumption of land and gross inequality among people in a region. Sprawl is deemed responsible for abandoned buildings, run-down neighborhoods, poor schools, pot-holed roads, polluted lakes and streams and feelings of alienation and disconnection among residents and their communities.

"We have caused the problem. It seems logical that we can deal with it," said Dan Piepszowski, director of Christian Service for the archdiocese, the division heading up the fight against sprawl. "We have to be uncomfortable with communities that are isolated racially or economically or socially. That's not a good healthy thing for the church," he added.

"Detroit was the envy of New York and Chicago 40 or 50 years ago," said Ann Serra, director of grants and metropolitan equity for the archdiocese, another leader in the effort. "There was a lot of money here because of manufacturing. No one would have thought Detroit could become what it is now. We were at the top."

According to Ms. Serra, Detroit began its downward economic spiral in the 1950s, when manufacturing began to move to the South as a means of avoiding high labor costs. The riot of 1967 accelerated the depopulation of the city. In the early 1970s bussing mandates to desegregate schools encouraged more movement of white Detroiters outward to a ring of suburbs around the city. Freeway construction accompanied that movement, and millions of dollars were spent in

---

building that accommodated an increase in automobile transportation and weakened the public transportation system's route scheduling and accessibility.

"There were restrictions on bus routes along racial lines," said Ms. Serra. White people did not want to ride a bus with black people, and buses did not go out to the suburbs where the jobs were. Black people who lived in the city

> *"We are a suburban nation."*—Dr. Robert Bullard, Clark Atlanta University

could not get a ride to their jobs. Indeed, one of the key issues surrounding sprawl is transportation. So the archdiocese is also working to promote a mass transit system in the southeastern Michigan region.

"The nation's transportation system is a kind of apartheid," said Dr. Robert Bullard, a sociologist from Clark Atlanta University in Atlanta, Ga., and a leading national expert on race and the environment. Mr. Bullard spoke last fall at the Conference on Living in Justice and Solidarity sponsored by the archdiocese. "It was set up to create racial, economic, social and geographical barriers in our communities."

"We are a suburban nation," said Mr. Bullard, citing that in 1990, 67 percent of new growth occurred in the metropolitan areas. Now 80 percent of new growth occurs in suburbs, where mostly white people live. In Detroit, 70 percent of the office space is located outside the city and out of reach of the many central city dwellers who need jobs and the transportation necessary to get to those jobs. One-third of the people do not own cars and most are poor and non-white. They rely on public transportation to get them to work, stores and social activities. But because of Detroit's limited public transportation system, only 2 percent of the population uses the system—as compared to cities like New York where 47 percent of the population get around on buses and trains.

The archdiocese has been educating Catholics about sprawl and its effects on the region since 1999. It hired Myron Orfield, president of the Metropolitan Area Research Corporation in Minneapolis and author of a groundbreaking book, *Metropolitics: Social Separation and Sprawl*, as a consultant on this project. He spoke at the fall conference, too.

"As population decreases, property values decrease, business disinvests in that community, and poorer people move in," said Mr. Orfield. But he said that the decline of Detroit goes much deeper. It turns out that the first ring of suburbs is declining and a second ring has been developing during the 1990s. According to Mr. Orfield, the Detroit metropolitan area has increased in land area by 30 percent, while the city's population—which peaked in 1950 at 2 million—is now half that size.

Mr. Orfield cites the example of Macomb County, north of Detroit, where the centrally located older suburban bedroom communities of Warren, Centerline, East Pointe and Fraser are losing middle-class residents to newer developments out on the edges of the county. Because these communities do not have much of an industrial or commercial tax base, they provide fewer resources and services per household and are experiencing physical deterioration. Poorer people are either left there or they are moving in.

"Part of the problem in Detroit is the historical pattern equating prosperity with movement away from the city to the suburbs," said Mr. Piepszowski. People left the city feeling pushed out because of crime, bad schools and drugs. They also feel pulled out because of government policies and incentives that favor growth.

Sprawl encourages local communities to adopt self-defeating behavior patterns that negatively affect economic development in their own backyards as well as those of their neighbors. Mr. Piepszowski noted that southeastern Michigan local governments compete with one another instead of cooperating for business development. This "creates an impediment to economic growth and prosperity for the whole region," he observed. Any talk about regional government and planning makes people suspicious that they might be asked to bail out Detroit, so they resist any attempts in that direction. Mr. Piepszowski said that resistance to regional approaches comes from the same pride and healthy parochialism that built these communities. But such an attitude also reduces the region's ability to attract businesses looking for an area that provides a support system of education, housing, a diverse labor pool and adequate transportation networks.

In fact, the history of regional approaches in Detroit has not been encouraging, including approaches advocated by the archdiocese. In the 1970s, for example, the archdiocese's support of bussing for the purpose of providing all races with equal opportunities for education helped to spark white flight to the suburbs. Today white people still blame black people for the decline of the city, while black people see sprawl as white people's problem. Mr. Piepszowski said that unless all the citizens of the region attack sprawl together, a backlash against regionalism might create more segregation.

"What drives Detroit is race," said the Rev. Steve Jones, pastor of First Baptist Church in Birmingham. Reverend Jones is part of a growing of interfaith coalition pastors that is working with the archdiocese to curb sprawl. Birmingham is one of the older suburbs of Detroit and home to high-income executives of the automobile companies. "You just can't get away from [race]," said the Rev. Jones. "It permeates everything we're about. Detroit is the most segregated metropolitan area [in the country]. It just passed Gary, Ind." He contends that race is one of the reasons why Detroiters have traditionally avoided building a mass transit system, too. "We can't imagine sitting on a bus with people different from us," he said. "We don't trust one another and we don't trust the differences. What's more, we don't have any practice [dealing with people who are different from ourselves]."

Cognizant of the racial divisions in the region, Mr. Piepszowski argues that people must learn more about others' faiths and lifestyles and learn to live with one another. "We Catholics have to be comfortable with diversity both internationally and domestically." Mr. Piepszowski points to Southfield as a gem of community diversity. An older, formerly white suburb in northwest Detroit, it now contains Armenians, African Americans, Chaldeans, Jews, and Russians living together. Such cities, he said, provide wonderful models of racial and cultural mixes.

The archdiocese's Christian Service Department relies on parishioners to assume the leadership for this new anti-sprawl ministry. It sees the ministry as another opportunity to build lay leadership. And laypeople are readily assuming their roles as leaders.

"We are getting a much better response from people as they become part of a public discourse," said Ann Serra, who remembers the hopelessness she witnessed during the first meetings of the new anti-sprawl ministry. In the suburban parishes she heard horrible stories about Coleman Young (the former black mayor of Detroit) and his policies, as well as people's fears about the migration and decline in the area. Now Ms. Serra conducts a dialogue with participants. She begins by first asking them why they chose the community they live in. Invariably they say, because of the schools, safety and lower taxes. No one has listed accessibility to shopping or highways. "What we are trying to do [through the sprawl issue] is build solidarity in the church," she said. "Everyone is learning as we dialogue. The people see that we're all Catholics, regardless of race, and that we have obligations to one another, whether we live in the city or the suburbs."

The archdiocese has been contacting all its 314 parishes to join in this ministry against sprawl and to promote a regional mass transit system in southeastern Michigan. It has also teamed up with a local community organizing group called Moses (Metropolitan Organizing Strategy Enabling Strength), which works with other religious congregations in the city and suburbs on this issue. Moses provides a training program that teaches citizens how to take responsibility and mobilize for change in a democratic way. Residents learn how to build citizen coalitions from a position of power and action.

"To be powerful is a good thing," said Bill O'Brien, executive director of Moses. "To be powerless is a scandal. Power is the ability to act. Through power we teach church leaders how to organize people and/or money." O'Brien said that people become empowered because they are in relationship with individuals and groups of people. "The church is a place of relationship and community. We provide people with a strategy to make that happen."

Archdiocesan leaders and other church organizers see the elections of 2002 as an opportunity to assert their power for a regional mass transit system. The state is about to undergo a huge turnover in leadership. Because of the state's term-limits law, there will be a change of governor as well as of 30 percent of its representatives and 70 percent of its state senators. Kwame Kilpatrick became Detroit's new mayor earlier this year after coming from the Michigan state legislature, where he sponsored a regional transportation bill.

"But the transportation network is just rubber and steel unless the relational pieces come into play," cautioned Mr. Piepszowski, who recognizes that there are still some political hold-outs against a mass transit system. "Transportation is a social delivery system. It's about people. Solving our transportation problems in the Detroit metropolitan area is one way to overcome inequality among people here. As Catholics, we come to our faith as a community. Catholic teaching is all about building community."

Ann Serra remains optimistic, too. "When you are connected, you see others' problems," she said. And relationships among church people, connections between the city and suburbs through this battle against sprawl—and for mass transit—are key to the archdiocese's hopes for promoting justice in the Detroit metropolitan area.

Antidotes to Sprawl Taking Many Forms[4]

By Dennis Hevesi
The New York Times, October 6, 2002

Of the 62 acres purchased two years ago by a developer in the town of Greenburgh, five miles north of New York City in Westchester County, only 10 are being developed—creating 86 attached homes while preserving the rest as wooded open space.

In Willingboro, N.J., 20 miles south of Trenton, a bankrupt and abandoned 1950s-style open-air shopping mall surrounded by what were once the cookie-cutter tracts of the third Levittown development is being resuscitated as a mixed-use community. The new Willingboro Town Center will have 210 three-story town houses concentrated in 30-unit enclaves, a library, a college building, an amphitheater overlooking a computerized 16-jet fountain, a supermarket, small retail stores and a pharmaceutical company's vast mail-order distribution plant, all in walking distance of bus and light-rail connections to Trenton, Camden and beyond.

To the roll call of often-conflicting parties engaged in the development process, both regionally and locally, the Greenburgh and Willingboro projects are prime examples of "smart growth."

It is a phrase and a movement and a cause for some contention—if only over what truly constitutes "smart growth"—that in recent years has permeated the dialogue among planners, politicians, environmentalists and public health advocates, not to mention developers.

It is everybody's remedy, although with varying doses and ingredients, for sprawl.

In essence, smart growth calls for the creation of higher-density communities within walking distance of transportation, shopping, schools and, where possible, jobs; or the redevelopment of underutilized and sometimes environmentally tainted sites, often in an urban core. All of which is intended to reduce automobile congestion—both to and from the suburbs, as well as within a city—promote walking, save open space and lower tax burdens by reducing the need for new infrastructure.

And while, like apple pie, it is hard to find anyone who opposes smart growth, some developers do raise questions: about the looseness of the definition—a legitimate concern given government support for some projects—about the balance between calls for land

---

preservation and the incessant need for more housing, and about land-use restrictions lowering property values, even if they curtail sprawl.

"Sprawl's been criticized for decades, from social critics dating back to the 1920s to the 1950s when suburban development really took off," said Don Chen, director of Smart Growth America, a non-profit advocacy group. "But even though the problem has been around for a while, it really has only taken off as an important political issue and market issue in the last 5 to 10 years."

In 1998, at a meeting of a group called the Smart Growth Network in Washington, advocates, planners and developers adopted a 10-point protocol calling for, among other things, "walkable neighborhoods," a variety of transportation choices, development directed toward existing communities, compact building design, mixed-use development and preservation of open space. Soon after, the National Governors Association adopted the principles.

In recent years, polls conducted by the Federal Highway Administration and the National Association of Realtors documented mounting public frustration with automobile congestion.

At the same time, researchers at the Centers for Disease Control and Prevention in Atlanta have conducted studies linking sprawl and traffic congestion to health problems among Americans, particularly obesity and cardiovascular disease due to lack of physical activity and fuel particulates in the air. "Basically, there are concerns that many health and environmental problems that we face are generated by the inefficient land-use patterns that market-driven, speculative sprawl has imprinted on the countryside," said Dr. Elliott Sclar, a professor of urban planning at Columbia University. "If your kid gets driven to school every day or if you go through the McDonald's drive-through for your Big Mac and a milk shake, you're going to have a hard time keeping the weight off."

For more than a decade, activists say, the New York State–chartered Empire State Development Corporation and the New Jersey Department of Environmental Protection have promoted projects incorporating smart-growth principles—largely through planning grants and tax incentives—a strategy more recently adopted by the Connecticut Development Authority.

State and local initiatives are currently supporting projects as varied as the reconfiguring of a fishing village on Long Island, the conversion of an 1856 lock factory in a rundown section of Norwalk, Conn., into office space—with new housing on adjacent lots—and, on a broader scale, the transfer of development rights from tracts of privately owned wilderness to parcels already zoned for construction.

Population trends are an impelling reason that smart growth has increasingly seeped into the development debate. "If you see demographics as destiny," said Mr. Chen, "it makes sense that there was an enormous suburban housing boom in the '50s to accommodate G.I.'s returning from the war front, and after that baby boomers, to address overcrowding in cities."

"Now," Mr. Chen continued, "as our demographic profile changes, there's increasing interest in in-town living, not only among young people, but also baby boomers as they become empty-nesters and start to retire. They see advantages to living in places with greater sense of community, more convenience. And that trend will be more pronounced over the next two decades."

The transformation of the old mall in Willingboro seems an indicator of the trend.

"It's being converted to a mixed-use town center where people can live, work, shop, study and walk," said Robert Stang, managing member of Renewal Realty, the developer of the Willingboro center.

What the developers found when they first surveyed the site in 1998 was nearly 600,000 square feet of retail space in abandoned buildings—including a Woolworth's, a Sears and an Acme supermarket—at the core of 56 acres and surrounded by "a sea of parking lots," Mr. Stang said. Surrounding that were 11,500 single-family homes.

"It was the third Levittown, built in the late '50s," Mr. Stang said. "Its name was changed because it was too close to the second Levittown, in Pennsylvania."

The mall had been a retail hub along Route 130—until Interstate 295 came through town in the mid-70s. The interstate, with big-box stores like Home Depot off its exit ramps, "sucked the retail out of the Route 130 corridor," Mr. Stang said.

His company, Mr. Stang said, paid the previous owner, who had long tried to attract a brand-name anchor store, $185,000 for all 56 acres. "I figured I could never get hurt," he said. "It would always be worth more than that."

With backing from the town, which took temporary title to the land, Renewal Realty received a $2 million low-interest loan to clean up the property. "The town had title, but we could acquire it for a dollar after we cleaned it up," Mr. Stang said.

Soon after, a master plan was drawn up very much in line with what Mr. Chen of Smart Growth America says is a growing trend toward replacing old malls "with entire P.U.D.'s—planned unit developments—meaning instead of building one house here, one house there, you build a community with residential, commercial, civic uses."

Willingboro's mayor, Paul Stephenson, is enthusiastic about what has arrived and soon will come. Merck-Medco, a subsidiary of the pharmaceutical company, took over a 100,000-square-foot existing building, added another 100,000 square feet and after opening its mail-order center "brought nearly 1,000 jobs into our community," Mayor Stephenson said. Burlington County College leased 19,000 square feet of existing space for a satellite classroom building. A supermarket and smaller retail stores have opened.

"The next piece," the mayor said, "is about 200 housing units that will primarily serve folks who have already raised their children, looking for transition from a big house to something more manageable." The first homes, for rental and later for sale, will be completed in about a year.

"Now," Mayor Stephenson said, "we take that mix and add our own investment—a library-media center, an amphitheater and a magnificent fountain."

"With the advent of the national trend toward people seeking gathering places within their communities," he said, "this is smart growth right on time."

The advent has actually been a long time coming.

"Smart growth is certainly a new term," said Dr. Sclar at Columbia, "but the concern with sprawl—meaning that the metropolitan area was growing in an unplanned pattern—goes back to the turn of the last century."

Professor Sclar cited Forest Hills Gardens in central Queens, built in 1909, as "basically what the smart-growth people are hoping to recreate in the 21st century."

Designed by Frederick Law Olmsted Jr., son of the landscape architect of Central Park, Forest Hills Gardens is a 142-acre community of large homes and row houses—many bearing the red-tile roofs, turrets and dormers in the English Tudor style—lining winding, tree-arched streets and spacious greenways.

> *"The concern with sprawl goes back to the turn of the last century."*—
> Dr. Elliott Sclar, Columbia University

"When you go from Station Square," Dr. Sclar said—referring to the Olde English town plaza where the Long Island Rail Road stops—"you walk under an archway into the greenway and there's smaller attached houses, one apartment building and the elementary school, P.S. 101. Then as you go further into the Gardens, the lot sizes and houses get bigger." One block north of the train station is Austin Street, lined with almost every conceivable sort of store, and Continental Avenue, where the subway to Manhattan stops.

"What the smart-growth people are talking about these days is basically to expand the supply of Forest Hills Gardenses," Dr. Sclar said. "The problem is the regionalists of the last century were never able to make this the standard, so you ended up with highways, strip malls, social isolation."

In 1929, an influential nonprofit group, the Regional Plan Association, asked Charles Dyer Norton, a famous planner, to help draft a development strategy for New York City. "When Norton came to New York, he realized such a movement here would have to be regional," said Thomas Wright, the current executive vice president of the association. "You couldn't plan for the city alone and address the fundamental issues because New York already was starting to function as a metropolitan region; people were already starting to commute."

The committee eventually created a comprehensive regional plan, calling for major investments in infrastructure, open-space preservation and new communities similar to Forest Hills Gardens. It included ambitious proposals for highways and railroads.

"The point is that the highways were built much more quickly than the railroads," Mr. Wright said. "Therefore, we developed in a more automobile-dependent manner."

And after World War II, the nation experienced the suburban boom, fueled by federal policies encouraging home ownership—the tax deduction for mortgages and the Interstate Highway Act—"which provided enormous funding for building the Interstates," he said, "while, at the same time, mass transit was essentially going bankrupt."

"How do you undo that?" Mr. Wright asked. "How do you retrofit sprawl to create communities that have the benefits of open space, diversity, opportunity?"

Some developers have some ideas.

Martin Ginsburg is president of GDC, which has built about 3,000 homes, most of them town houses, in Westchester, Rockland and Fairfield Counties. In Greenburgh, N.Y., the company bought 62 acres of green space for $5 million and named it—appropriately—Wyldwood.

"There was a strong movement in the community to keep it open space," Mr. Ginsburg said, "but they couldn't raise the money to buy all 62 acres, so we came up with a compromise." With financing assistance from the state, Westchester County and the nonprofit Open Space Institute, the town bought 42 of the acres to be preserved as open space.

"We ended up developing 86 units on 10 of the remaining 20 acres," Mr. Ginsburg said. "The result was less development, but some development, on only 10 of the 62 acres."

In a more urban setting—along a rundown riverfront stretch in Norwalk, Conn.—Kim Morque's company, Spinnaker Development, has converted an old lock factory into 104,000 square feet of "nontraditional office space."

"It's open; exposed-beam ceilings, brick walls," Mr. Morque said. "Tenants devise their space according to their needs."

From 1856 to the mid-1950s, the three-story building was the Norwalk Lock Company. In recent decades, until Spinnaker bought it for $3.25 million in March 2000, it housed "small manufacturers, carpenters, artists, even a sailmaker," Mr. Morque said.

"This is smart growth because we are recycling land, taking industrial sites and brownfields and creating new projects," he said. "And because we're using an existing building, we're utilizing existing utilities—water, electrical, sewage—and not building new infrastructure."

The building is five blocks from the South Norwalk train station. "About 250 people work there," Mr. Morque said. "They can walk to lunch, shop on nearby Washington Street. Many of them live in the area."

Across the street, Mr. Morque said, plans call for construction of 10 condominiums, 3,000 square feet of commercial and 5,000 square feet of street-level retail space. "Then we have plans for 200 apartments and a hotel on the site to the east," he said.

For Jim Tripp and Eric Kulleseid, two prominent land-preservation activists in the New York area, Mr. Morque's downtown Norwalk redevelopment and even Mr. Ginsburg's limited development on 62 acres in Greenburgh are significant examples of smart growth. But their sights are set on far more ambitious efforts to limit sprawl and protect vast tracts of open space.

"It may be smart growth on a microscale to cluster development on a fraction of the parcel and set aside the remainder for open space," said Mr. Tripp, general counsel for Environmental Defense, a national nonprofit organization. "But you can take that notion and look at the whole metropolitan area, much more macroscale, and ask yourself: what large pieces of land do we want to protect that are in private ownership, where we could redirect development to other more appropriate places?"

Mr. Tripp and Mr. Kulleseid, who is the New York State director of the nonprofit Trust for Public Land, believe it is vital to preserve, among other swaths of wilderness, up to 500,000 privately owned acres of forest in the undulating highlands that stretch through northern New Jersey, across the Hudson and into Connecticut, as well as 100,000 acres in Suffolk County called the Long Island Pine Barrens.

Mr. Kulleseid's group is one of a network of organizations that specialize in finding funds to compensate landowners who sign easements agreeing never to allow development on their property. "We need forests and wetlands because they give us clean water, places to be physical and not just denizens of the local mall," Mr. Kulleseid said. And, viewing forests as akin to lungs, he said, "They soak up greenhouse gases and give back oxygen."

Mr. Tripp of Environmental Defense is also chairman of the Pine Barrens Credit Clearinghouse, an arm of the Long Island Pine Barrens Commission. The commission was created by state legislation to preserve about 100,000 acres of pitch pine and oak forest in the sandy soil that forms a sort of spine through the Suffolk County towns of Brookhaven, Riverhead and Southhampton.

Under the plan, two tools are used to protect privately owned land. One is outright acquisition, for which the county and state have spent about $100 million. The other is the transfer of development rights.

Under the transfer program, private landowners in the core of the Pine Barrens can be allocated development rights based on the amount of land they own and the applicable zoning. If, for example, the zoning is one house per acre, the landowner is entitled to one credit, which can be sold to any developer who owns land where the three towns have designated a receiving area for higher-density development.

"The developer knows that rather than building one house for every two acres, for example, he or she could build a house on every acre," Mr. Tripp said. "What the landowner in the Pine Barrens must do to obtain this right is record a conservation easement on the property. They retain the title, but they can't develop it."

"And this does not cost the public a cent," he said. "The saving of that land, in effect, has been paid for by developers who find it economically worthwhile to build higher-density development."

A bit farther east, at the tip of Long Island's South Shore, local officials and developers hope to devise a smart-growth plan for the tiny fishing village of Montauk in the town of East Hampton.

"Growth has been constrained by outdated zoning and by a single loop road in and out of the dock area," said Jonathan F. P. Rose, president of the Jonathan Rose Companies. Mr. Rose's firm has been asked to draft a plan "that allows businesses to grow, creates housing and rationalizes traffic."

Rather than allowing development to spread, the key might be the renovation of a half-dozen ramshackle hotels, said Town Supervisor Jay Schneiderman. "There's the fishing pier, and right across from it you have this blighted area, all these boarded-up buildings," he said.

"The community is facing a challenge to provide adequate housing for workers," Mr. Schneiderman continued, "and one thought is to create employee housing in this area, and, at the same time, some new shops and offices. Of course, there would be pedestrian areas, open space. And there might be apartments over the shops."

Whatever plan is adopted should retain, said Mr. Rose, the developer, "the funky nautical character of the place, and not make it a sanitized touristy resort."

Supervisor Schneiderman said, "All ideas are on the table."

II. Trends in Development

Editor's Introduction

Sprawl is rapidly reshaping the American urban environment. Every year more rural farmland is being seized for development: between 1990 and 2000, more than 17,000 square miles of land that was formerly rural reached suburban or urban densities, an amount more than twice the size of New Jersey. Once-vibrant main streets of small towns have emptied and eroded over time as chains such as Wal-Mart and Home Depot—called "big-box" retailers for their boxy, unadorned design—develop superstores on cheaper land outside of town. The last few decades have seen the proliferation of edge cities, a term coined by Joel Garreau in 1991 to describe these vast new urban centers that don't look anything like traditional cities. Also known as "boomburgs," they are in essence suburbs that have been detached from cities and become urban centers in their own right, only more spread out. They feature gleaming office towers intermixed with vast parking lots, shopping malls, subdivisions, fast-food restaurants, and gas stations.

Americans respond to these changes in different ways. Many view them as a sign of progress, the natural result of allowing individual choices and market forces to determine the shape of cities. The abundance of undeveloped, cheap land, they argue, allows for more affordable housing, making possible the American ideal of owning a large home with a grassy front lawn in a safe cul-de-sac and the ability to drive wherever one wants.

Others see only "soulless" suburban developments, lacking organization and aesthetic appeal and inimical to a happy and healthy life. This view is held by proponents of New Urbanism, a movement pioneered by the husband-and-wife architectural team of Andres Duany and Elizabeth Plater-Zyberk. In 1980 Duany and Plater-Zyberk created Seaside, a resort development in Florida that offered a new type of community, specifically built to resemble the old-fashioned small town of America's past, with historic architectural styles and houses with porches lining narrow streets within walkable distance of downtown shopping areas, parks, and public squares. Initially regarded as a novel experiment, Seaside was soon a success, with property values increasing tenfold in the first few years. *Time* magazine praised it as one of the 10 great design achievements of the 1980s. Since then New Urbanism has grown into a popular movement that many real-estate theorists consider to be on the leading edge of urban design.

This chapter begins with an article by Duany and Plater-Zyberk, "The Traditional Neighborhood & Suburban Sprawl," in which they present the guidelines they follow in building New Urbanist communities and the New Urbanist criticisms of typical suburban development. This is followed by an article by Deborah K. Dietsch, "The New Neotraditionalists," which examines recent variations of New Urbanist developments, some of which adhere strictly to the guidelines while others appropriate them to varying degrees. Dietsch points out the successes as well as the failures of these developments. A dissenting view of New Urbanism is found in the third article, "Plan Obsolescence," wherein Rick Henderson, managing editor of *Reason*, and Adrian T. Moore, director of economic studies at the Reason Public Policy Institute, present an interview with Peter Gordon, a professor of planning and economics at the University of Southern California. Gordon argues that sprawl and car-oriented development should not be seen as problems to be solved, since they in fact represent consumer choice. Moreover, he claims that development should be driven by market forces and not public policy.

Growing metropolitan regions are increasingly taking measures to combat sprawl. Among them is Portland, Oregon, considered by many to be a posterchild for growth management. In "Portland's Green Peace: At Play in the Fields of Urban Planning," Jay Walljasper, editor at large of the *Utne Reader*, outlines a few of Portland's efforts, from its light-rail transit system to its Urban Growth Boundary, a line beyond which development is prohibited, thereby limiting sprawl and retaining investment within the city proper. Walljasper also discusses Portland's unique form of elected regional government, Metro, and the role of activists in city planning.

In "Anti-Box Rebellion," Jonathan Walters offers a look at regional planning and community involvement taking place on a smaller scale, in the township of Hatfield, Massachusetts, population 3,249. In a drama familiar to small towns across the country, the retailer Home Depot, seeking to build one of its superstores in the area, met with resistance from the community. Superstore development has proven a hotbed of controversy in the 1990s, with proponents crediting the stores with supplying jobs and tax revenues, and critics claiming they increase traffic, undermine local small businesses, and deprive towns of their individuality.

Development patterns are also changing in edge cities. Some are beginning to incorporate features usually associated with smart growth, as Jonathan Barnett records in "Turning Edge Cities into Real Cities." In places like Addison, Texas, walkable, mixed-use developments with urban squares and concealed parking are beginning to crop up amidst the highways and office parks. Barnett argues that this is in part a response to the fact that "many of these highway-oriented developments are rapidly becoming a problem because they no longer make money for their owners." He suggests that shopping-mall redevelopment and new transit systems can help edge cities manage growth more efficiently.

In the final article of this section, "Poor Area Heart of Plan," Nicole White looks at one of the ways in which large cities are seeking to revive poorer neighborhoods by encouraging new development. In Overtown, Miami, a formerly prosperous black neighborhood that is now struggling, legislators are considering designating the area an "urban revitalization zone." The proposed plan, according to White, seeks to lure new businesses to the area by exempting them from paying or collecting sales tax, and it would require that 20 percent of their workforce be hired from within the neighborhood.

The Traditional Neighborhood and Suburban Sprawl[1]

By Andres Duany and Elizabeth Plater-Zyberk
Conscious Choice, April 2001

The congested, fragmented, unsatisfying suburban sprawl and the disintegrating urban centers of today are not merely products of laissez-faire nor the inevitable results of mindless greed. They are thoroughly planned to be as they are: the direct result of zoning and subdivision ordinances zealously administered by planning departments.

If the results are dismaying, it is because the model of the city being projected is dismal. These ordinances dictate three criteria for urbanism: the free and rapid flow of traffic, parking in quantity, and the rigorous separation of building use. The result of these criteria is that automobile traffic and its landscape have become the central, unavoidable experience of the public realm.

The traditional pattern of walkable, mixed-use neighborhoods has been inadvertently prohibited by current ordinances. Thus, designers find themselves in the ironic situation of being forbidden from building in the manner of our admired historic places. One cannot propose a new Annapolis, Marblehead, or Key West, without seeking substantial variances from current codes.

Thus, there are two types of urbanism available. The neighborhood, which was the model in North America from the first settlements to the second World War, and Suburban Sprawl, which has been the model since then. They are similar in their initial capacity to accommodate people and their activities; the principal difference is that Suburban Sprawl contains environmental, social, and economic deficiencies that inevitably choke sustained growth.

The neighborhood has the following physical attributes:

- The neighborhood is a comprehensive planning increment: when clustered with others, it becomes a town; when standing free in the landscape, it becomes a village. The neighborhood varies in population and density to accommodate localized conditions.

- The neighborhood is limited in size so that a majority of the population is within a five-minute walking distance of its center (a quarter-mile). The needs of daily life are theoretically available within this area. This center provides an

1. Reprinted with the permission of Andres Duany and Elizabeth Plater-Zyberk from the April 2001 issue of *Conscious Choice* magazine (*www.ConsciousChoice.com*).

excellent location for a transit stop, convenience work places, retail, community events, and leisure activities.

- The streets are laid out in a network, so that there are alternate routes to most destinations. This permits most streets to be smaller with slower traffic and to have parking, trees, sidewalks, and buildings. They are equitable for both vehicles and pedestrians.

- The streets are spatially defined by a wall of buildings that front the sidewalk in a disciplined manner, uninterrupted by parking lots.

- The buildings are diverse in function, but compatible in size and in disposition on their lots. There is a mixture of houses (large and small), outbuildings, small apartment buildings, shops, restaurants, offices, and warehouses.

- Civic buildings (schools, meeting halls, theaters, churches, clubs, museums, etc.) are often placed on squares or at the termination of street vistas. By being built at important locations, these buildings serve as landmarks.

- Open space is provided in the form of specialized squares, playgrounds, and parks and, in the case of villages, greenbelts.

Suburban sprawl has quite different physical attributes:

- Sprawl is disciplined only by isolated "pods," which are dedicated to single uses such as "shopping centers," "office parks," and "residential clusters." All of these are inaccessible from each other except by car. Housing is strictly segregated in large clusters containing units of similar cost, hindering socioeconomic diversity.

- Sprawl is limited only by the range of the automobile which easily forms cachment areas for retail, often exceeding fifty miles.

- There is a high proportion of cul-de-sacs and looping streets within each pod. Through traffic is possible only by means of a few "collector" streets which, consequently, become easily congested.

- Vehicular traffic controls the scale and form of space, with streets being wide and dedicated primarily to the automobile. Parking lots typically dominate the public space.

- Buildings are often highly articulated, rotated on their lots, and greatly set back from streets. They are unable to create spatial definition or sense of place. Civic buildings do not normally receive distinguished sites.

- Open space is often provided in the form of "buffers," "pedestrian ways," "berms," and other ill-defined residual spaces.

The neighborhood has several positive consequences:

- By bringing most of the activities of daily living into walking distance, everyone (especially the elderly and the young) gains independence of movement.
- By reducing the number and length of automobile trips, traffic congestion is minimized, the expenses of road construction are limited, and air pollution is reduced.
- By providing streets and squares of comfortable scale with defined spatial quality, neighbors, walking, can come to know each other and to watch over their collective security.
- By providing appropriate building concentrations at easy walking distances from transit stops, public transit becomes a viable alternative to the automobile.
- By providing a full range of housing types and workplaces, age and economic classes are integrated and the bonds of an authentic community are formed.
- By providing suitable civic buildings and spaces, democratic initiatives are encouraged and the balanced evolution of society is facilitated.

Suburban sprawl has several negative consequences:

- By assuming that the people will drive to and from all activities, the need for large streets and parking lots becomes a self-fulfilling prophecy. The exhaust emissions resulting from such trips are the single greatest source of air pollution in the United States.
- By the construction of an excessive asphalt infrastructure, the natural landscape is destroyed. Each automobile not only generates roadways, but also requires a paved parking place at the dwelling, another at the workplace, and yet another at the shopping center.
- By consigning the bulk of the available public budget to pay for asphalt infrastructure, the human infrastructure of good schools, post offices, fire stations, meeting halls, cultural buildings, and affordable housing is starved.

Certain classes of citizens who suffer particularly from the pattern of suburban sprawl include:

- The middle class, who are forced into multiple automobile ownership. The average yearly cost of car ownership is

$5,000, which is the equivalent of a $50,000 mortgage payment. The possibility of owning one less car is the single most important subsidy that can be provided towards affordable housing. By forbidding mixed-use areas, the investment of personal time in the activity of commuting is mandatory. A person who drives two hours a day spends the equivalent of eight working weeks a year in the car.

- The young, below the legal driving age, who are dependent on adults for their social needs. They are bused to schools, from which they cannot walk, and isolated at home until their working parents arrive. The alternative is to relegate one parent to a career as the child's chauffeur. The single family house with the yard is a good place for childhood only if it is structured as part of a neighborhood. Within these, the child can walk or bicycle to school, to play, to the store, to the movies, and to friends' houses.

- The elderly, who lose their self-sufficiency once they lose their drivers' licenses. Healthy senior citizens who may continue to live independently within a neighborhood are otherwise consigned to specialized retirement communities where their daily needs are met at great cost.

Suburban sprawl usually accommodates the correct balance of work places, living places, schools, and open space in what appears to be proximity. However, proximity is not enough; the detailing of the public space to accommodate the pedestrian is also necessary:

- Buildings must be aligned along streets and squares. The current fashion of staggering or rotating buildings hinders the creation of public space defined by the buildings.

- Trees along streets must also be aligned in a disciplined manner. This is particularly important to remedy spaces when over-large setbacks cannot be avoided. Picturesque planting patterns should be reserved for parks and squares, not for streets and avenues.

- Parallel parking must be provided on most streets. A layer of parked cars protects the pedestrians from traffic psychologically. Parking lots, when they are needed, should be placed to the rear of buildings to avoid the gaps that make sidewalks uninteresting to use. House lots, if less than fifty feet wide, should be provided with alleys so that garage doors do not overwhelm the street facades.

- At intersections, the radius at the curb should not exceed fifteen feet. This maintains a viable pedestrian crossing distance and reduces the speed of automobiles making the turn.

- High-capacity streets within urbanized areas should have the geometry of avenues, not of highways. Highways are unpleasant for pedestrians and deteriorate adjacent building value, while avenues are compatible with buildings and people. Highways should be reserved for the countryside and be built without strip development.

In a neighborhood, affordable housing occurs naturally and in a highly integrated manner. This is achieved by the following means:

- The affordable housing looks like the market-rate housing, using similar exterior materials, windows, and building forms. Affordable housing is not segregated and is never clustered in large numbers. A good ratio is one affordable unit to ten market-rate units.

- Housing is provided above retail establishments. This type of dwelling can be provided for the cost of construction alone, because the cost of land can be assigned to the retail component of the building.

- Garage apartments or cottages are available in the back-yards of single family houses. These rental units, of limited size, provide extremely affordable housing that is interspersed with market-rate housing. This also allows teenagers to stay at home and the elderly to live with their families.

Current codes monitor only traffic flow, parking counts, the segregation of building use, and the safeguard of wetlands. New codes must be written that include effective provisions for the neighborhood, which is human habitat in all its complexity.

The New Neotraditionalists[2]

By Deborah K. Dietsch
The Washington Post, September 8, 2001

Behind the white picket fence in front of his house, Don Naideck is chatting about his new patio with next-door neighbor Murray Toomey, who stands in his yard just a few feet away. Both recently bought four-bedroom houses in King Farm, a 430-acre development in Rockville designed according to a planning concept called traditional neighborhood development, also known as neotraditional or new urbanist development.

In this type of suburb, houses are arranged closely together and near the street. Each is designed in a slightly different traditional style with an old-fashioned porch in the front and a garage in the back. White picket fences flank brick sidewalks leading to parks, a community center and a nearby shopping center. These elements are intended to imitate the village charm of Georgetown or Annapolis, and foster the very neighborliness being shared by Toomey and Naideck in the heat of a summer afternoon.

"This is a way to be more connected to people than living in a mini-castle on a two-acre lot," said Naideck, 46, a business broker who moved to King Farm a year ago from a Silver Spring town house with his wife, Linor, and their two young children. With its mix of single-family houses, town houses, condominiums and rental apartments, along with stores, restaurants, recreational facilities and an office park, King Farm is one of the more ambitious traditional neighborhood developments (TNDs) now being built in the Washington suburbs. Others include Lakelands and Fallsgrove in Montgomery County; Belmont Greene, South Riding and Brambleton in Loudoun County and Belmont Bay in Prince William County. (There is no relationship between Belmont Greene and Belmont Bay; both neighborhoods take their names from local historical features.)

These new developments, all of which are under construction or about to break ground, represent the second generation of TNDs to be built on large suburban tracts. They loosely follow a type of neighborhood design pioneered by Miami architects Andres Duany and Elizabeth Plater-Zyberk in the 1980s. The planning method harkens back to older, small towns for inspiration. It aims to replace the typical subdivision of cookie-cutter homes on cul-de-sacs with more closely knit communities where people can live, work and shop.

---

2. Article by Deborah K. Dietsch from *The Washington Post* September 8, 2001. Copyright © Deborah K. Dietsch. Reprinted with permission.

Duany and Plater-Zyberk first experimented with new urbanism at Seaside, a resort community in the Florida panhandle. In 1988, they were hired to apply their new planning ideas to a year-round neighborhood in the suburb of a major city—Kentlands in Gaithersburg.

Developer Joseph Alfandre bought the 356-acre Kent farm off Route 28 and wanted to build a new type of

Locally, developers and builders are giving new urbanism a new twist.

neighborhood. Duany and Plater-Zyberk developed a plan that called for 1,600 homes, town houses and apartments in five neighborhoods, an elementary school, office space, a community building and a regional shopping center. Narrow streets were laid out in a city-style grid with brick sidewalks to encourage walking. Houses were designed in traditional styles and materials. Garages with second-story "granny flats" were relegated to rear alleys to encourage activity in the front yards and sidewalks.

Securing approvals from local officials unfamiliar with such unconventional plans proved difficult and time-consuming, however. Elements of the plan—a traffic circle, narrow streets and office buildings—were rejected. Home builders, too, were not used to the stringent design guidelines for single-family and town houses. "They were really strict with historic precedents," said Eric Tovar, president of Churchill Homes, one of the builders in Kentlands and King Farm. "All the details had to be authentic. You couldn't mix Georgian with Victorian."

For the home buyer, the exacting traditional design of the houses and the neighborhood translated into higher prices. Home sales were slow and the developer of the retail component withdrew from the project. In 1991, at a time when the building industry was struggling with slow sales, Alfandre gave control of Kentlands to his lender, Chevy Chase Bank, which finished the project.

Despite these setbacks, Kentlands was completed largely according to its original vision. And it has inspired developers across the nation to construct communities according to the old-town principles of new urbanism. About 400 traditional neighborhood developments have been completed or are under construction throughout the country, said Steven Bodzin, spokesman for the Congress for the New Urbanism, a San Francisco-based advocacy and research group.

Locally, developers and builders are giving new urbanism a new twist. They are combining aspects of neotraditional planning with more conventional subdivision design to create denser neighborhoods with stores and community amenities.

Now being completed next door to Kentlands is a 343-acre TND called Lakelands, which has its own shopping street, corner store and community amenities. Though it was master-planned by Duany and Plater-Zyberk to blend into Kentlands, the newer neighborhood is being built by Natelli Communities of Gaithersburg and Classic Community Corp. of Bethesda to appeal to a wider range of buyers.

"One of the things that we've tried for is greater design flexibility in housing types and materials," said Steve Eckert, president of Classic Community Corp. "Kentlands was set up for small, boutique builders and higher priced homes. We needed to attract merchant builders and address a broader market."

Newer TNDs have also loosened up the strict planning restrictions imposed at Kentlands. South Riding and Brambleton in Loudoun County and Fallsgrove in Rockville are only partially designed as traditional neighborhoods. When completed, town houses and smaller single-family houses with rear garages will be concentrated nearer to shopping and offices, while more typical suburban houses on bigger lots will be on the periphery.

"It gives the community a mix of ingredients that attract a wider range of buyers," said Greg Cox, development manager of Fallsgrove in Rockville. Though the 256-acre TND has yet to complete a model home, it has sold 227 of its planned 1,300 houses and expects to complete the first units in January.

Even more-orthodox TNDs are playing with the rules. Streets are curved rather than gridded in Belmont Greene, a 504-home development now under construction in Loudoun County. In Lakelands, some of the single-family houses have garages on the sides rather than in alleys at the rear.

The choice of materials for builders in these communities has also been broadened to reduce construction costs. Instead of requiring Kentlands' all-natural palette of wood clapboard, cedar roof shakes and copper gutters, newer TNDs allow for vinyl siding, asphalt roof shingles and other less expensive elements.

"You still get traditional architecture without the added expense and maintenance headaches," Eckert said.

Delia McCormick, a real estate broker with Long and Foster in Potomac Village, said houses in Lakelands sold for $338,000 to $618,000 over the past year, as compared with $345,000 to $680,000 in Kentlands.

But even in newer TNDs, houses are more expensive than those in conventional subdivisions. A statistical analysis conducted by George Washington University professors Mark Eppli and Charles Tu found that single-family houses in Kentlands and three other neotraditional neighborhoods command prices that are 4 percent to 25 percent higher than for comparable models in surrounding communities.

Builders of TNDs attribute the higher home prices to higher costs of site development. "You're talking about building a mini-city," said Mark Gregg of Penrose Group, the main developer of King Farm. "It's far more complex than the standard suburban development.

There is a much denser infrastructure—more utilities, roads, land-scaping, lights—and you're building the neighborhood out over a longer period of time."

Though TNDs are billed as offering stores and offices within walking distance, the commercial components often take years to be built—or do not ever happen. In Loudoun County's Belmont Forest, a TND developed by Kentlands' Alfandre, retail was never built, apart from a corner store that closed. To shop for groceries, Heather DeVido, a stay-at-home mom who has lived in the community since 1995, drives to a shopping center in Ashburn Village five miles away. "We were sold a concept that didn't happen," she said.

"There are developers who are trying to mimic elements of TND without embracing the real totality of them," Eckert said. "Belmont Forest failed miserably because it didn't have a big enough mix of product to make it a place. It was a subdivision masquerading as a TND."

Now Belmont Forest is being incorporated into Belmont Greene, an adjacent TND being developed by Waterford/Bouwfonds. The new neighborhood is planned to offer shopping and offices, and many of the community amenities, such as swimming pools and tennis courts, missing from the older development. Developer Jan A. Zachariasse of Waterford/Bouwfonds said the chances of successfully attracting home buyers and businesses to Belmont Greene are greater now because of access from the Dulles Greenway, which did not exist when Belmont Forest was developed.

Other developers of new TNDs are trying to make good on the promise of a small-town atmosphere by offering stores and amenities up front. Though only half built, King Farm has a Safeway, convenience store, bank, dry cleaner and other businesses for its residents. Lakelands has a shopping district with an art deco-inspired movie theater and diner, and a corner store in its residential district. Belmont Bay, now being built on the banks of the Occoquan River in Woodbridge, has opened a 150-slip marina.

Town greens, parks and recreational centers in these communities are designed to offset smaller lots and tightly spaced houses. "We try not to focus on the density, but the sense of the neighborhood," said Kim Adams, marketing manager of Brambleton, a 2,000-acre development near Dulles Airport that is to break ground this fall. Seventy percent of the community is designed as a TND and will offer a golf course, a conference center and walking trails in addition to retail and office space.

TND advocates argue that by situating shops, services and work places within walking distance, traffic congestion can be reduced. Visits to these communities reveal, however, that people rarely walk to shop or work. "There's not as much walking as intended," admits William Gilligan, vice president of Toll Brothers, now completing South Riding in Loudoun County. "People walk their dogs, but they don't walk to the supermarket and carry their groceries home."

Toomey, 44, who lives only a short stroll away from the King Farm shopping center, said he and his wife, Elizabeth, do not walk to shop and both drive to work. "I moved here because of the close-in location and the house, not the walking," he said.

At Fallsgrove, builders are offering financial incentives to encourage homeowners to walk and bike to work. Renters who commute a mile or less from their homes are eligible to deduct $500 off the first month's rent; home prices for owners living close to work are reduced by $1,000 to $2,000 depending on the size of the house.

For suburbanites used to houses on quarter-acre lots and cul-de-sacs, the higher density of TNDs—up to 7 to 10 units per acre—can be a turn-off. "There are a lot of people who would never consider communities like King Farm because of closeness of the houses," Long and Foster's McCormick said.

"Density is a dirty word," Eckert said. "It's associated with more traffic and congestion." Concern over increased density has led residents in Fairfax County and other suburban communities to protest mixed-use, high-rise development plans around Metro stations. This

---

"We want new communities to be patterned on historic communities with a mix of dwelling types, a pedestrian emphasis, and open space."—Julie Pastor, planning director

---

summer, for example, McLean residents voiced opposition to a Duany-designed mini-city of apartment buildings, shopping center, hotel, offices and restaurants near the future transit stop at Tysons Corner.

But as states and counties consider ways of taming sprawl, they are rewriting zoning laws to make it easier to build TNDs and other types of mixed-use, high-density neighborhoods in the suburbs. "The problem is that this kind of traditional neighborhood development has been illegal," said John W. Frece, communications director for the Maryland Governor's Office of Smart Growth. "It would be really hard to build Annapolis today. The streets are too narrow, the uses are too mixed, the setbacks aren't set back enough."

To help jurisdictions change their zoning laws, the Maryland Department of Planning has drafted a model code to encourage "smart" communities such as TNDs. "We aren't imposing these codes on local governments," Frece said. "But the governor will set up financial incentives that will be available to those jurisdictions that adopt these models or something similar."

As part of its newly revised comprehensive plan, Loudoun County has also endorsed TND-style communities as a way of controlling growth. "We're in the process of revising our zoning ordinance to better implement the design objectives of the traditional concepts," said Julie Pastor, the county's director of planning. "We want new communities to be patterned on historic communities with a mix of dwelling types, a pedestrian emphasis, and open space."

Like many developers, Pastor advocates a more flexible approach to TNDs than the Kentlands model. "What we found was general resistance to Duany-styled communities. Rather than being so strict, we are looking at combining elements of both traditional and suburban styles to achieve a high-quality cluster development."

As to the future growth of denser, town-styled suburbs, even developers of TNDs said the concept has its limits. "I don't know many communities that are running out to embrace urbanness," Eckert said. "Building density out here is going to be an ongoing debate."

Plan Obsolescence[3]

By Rick Henderson and Adrian T. Moore
Reason, June 1998

Life in America's suburbs is under attack. In journals ranging from *The Nation, The Atlantic Monthly*, and *Utne Reader* to *The American Enterprise* and *The Weekly Standard*, critics of suburbia argue that policies implemented since World War II—from the home-mortgage income tax deduction to subsidies for automobile operation to inflexible zoning laws—have lured Americans away from traditional downtowns and urban neighborhoods into soulless suburbs, where a landscape littered with strip malls and tract housing makes it nearly impossible for people to form genuine communal bonds with their neighbors. Contemporary suburbanites are condemned, in the words of the left-leaning *L.A. Weekly*, to "a future of endless sprawl and equally endless commutes."

To save suburban dwellers from this hellish existence, urban planners have devised massive subway construction projects, controls on the development of neighborhoods with single-family homes, "mixed-use" zoning districts that allow commercial operations to coexist with residences, and "urban growth boundaries" that have made it illegal to build homes or locate businesses on the outskirts of such cities as Portland, Oregon.

Enter Peter Gordon, a professor of planning and economics at the University of Southern California's School of Urban Planning and Development. For nearly three decades, Gordon, along with his USC colleague Harry Richardson, has challenged conventional views about gridlock and sprawl, finding that the data don't match the received wisdom: "Suburbanization" is not an artifact of late-20th-century America but a process that has unfolded as long as people have possessed the means to travel and relocate. Commute times are no longer than they were 15 years ago. Individuals are finding the types of living arrangements they prefer. And while Los Angeles-style sprawl is vilified in the traditional planning literature, as well as in most popular accounts of urban life, Los Angeles has the highest population density of any major metropolitan area in the country.

Gordon, who received his Ph.D. from the University of Pennsylvania, has published dozens of articles in popular publications and peer-reviewed journals. He is co-editor of *Planning and Markets*, a new online publication that focuses on land-use and transportation issues (*www-pam.usc.edu*). While he may be considered a lightning rod in the planning community, in person he's gentle and patient, hardly the sort of firebrand his heretical views suggest.

Reason Managing Editor Rick Henderson and Adrian T. Moore, director of economic studies at the Reason Public Policy Institute, interviewed Gordon at his Brentwood home in March.

Reason: There is a pervasive argument among traditional planners that compact cities built around a traditional downtown are intrinsically good. While cities once developed around transit centers, raw materials sites, or natural harbors, contemporary cities seem to be more the artificial creations of planners. What has happened?

Gordon: Compact cities are archaic forms, and they are not coming back. When you study the economics of location, all the textbook models say a firm wants to locate near the urban core or other advantageous sites, and workers must make their living arrangements so that they are close to their jobs. That may be the way it was once upon a time.

But all these firms have become much more footloose. And they go where the workers want to live. The orientation has flip-flopped. Even manufacturing businesses are no longer locked into specific sites, so they have more locational choices. They want to go where the labor force wants to go. The workers and their families want to live where the land is cheap and the air is clean and the schools are good and there are high amenities and so forth. There's a lot more spatial flexibility than ever before, and the consequences are pretty benign.

People don't have to live near work. They can be near good schools if they want to be without paying the price in longer-duration commutes. If you make travel less expensive, there will be more travel.

Reason: You've shown that the average-duration commute has stayed the same over the past 15 years or so. Why does everyone believe that traffic congestion is getting worse?

Gordon: What's interesting is how little congestion there is. If you take a resident of any large foreign city like Tokyo and transplant him or her to Los Angeles, they think they've died and gone to heaven, because the commutes are less than half, on average, here than they are there. Something like 10 percent of the people nationwide commute more than 40 minutes one way. There is a lot of self-correction going on. For 1995, the average automobile commute in L.A. was 23.5 minutes one way.

People are part of a spontaneous order. I think it's not only pessimistic but even ignorant to believe that people are going to sit tight while their lives go to hell. That's never happened. Even where the commuting distances have increased, the trip durations have not, which means commuting speeds are up. It is the opposite of impending gridlock, and it means people can have their cake and eat it, too.

Reason: So why don't people in Tokyo correct in the same way Angelenos do?

Gordon: Many Japanese choose long train commutes because they have a much smaller scope of trade-offs available. Automobile travel is much more expensive [in Japan]. Land doesn't change hands as frequently. There are all kinds of things standing in the way of the fluidity that we're used to.

Reason: You're a critic of the New Urbanism, which is the hot thing in the planning profession. Here's how Alan Ehrenhalt describes the principles of New Urbanism in *Governing* magazine: "The automobile, and four decades of building homes, streets and suburbs for the automobile's convenience, were draining American places of the community and intimacy that human beings naturally desire." The New Urbanists claim that people want neighborhoods with tree-lined streets, and parks and shops all within walking distance of homes. What's wrong with that?

> *The development of neighborhoods by private developers is driven by markets, not by public policy.*

Gordon: I think the development of neighborhoods by private developers is driven by markets, not by public policy. People are getting the neighborhoods they want. And I trust that competing developers are reading the trade-offs that you and I are willing to make and that those trade-offs include our demand for community. Our demands for community are met in many ways. We can use the automobile [to meet those demands], or we can even use the Internet.

People are getting a sense of community in the neighborhoods we have. We know that 20 percent of all trips by automobile are for work, 20 percent are for shopping, and 60 percent are for things I would call social. The U.S. Department of Transportation uses categories like family/personal business, school, church, visits to relatives, and other social or recreational uses, but you could easily call all these social or "community" trips.

New Urbanism is heavy on intervention, and it's tied into the "civil society," or communitarian, discussion. It dances around defining whether there's a problem with the way we live and says, "There's a problem—automobile use—and we have a solution." I'm not sure we all agree there's a problem. And it's a long shot to say that there's a design fix and we know what that design fix is.

Reason: Conservatives such as Karl Zinsmeister at the American Enterprise Institute have become big boosters of New Urbanism. They argue that the fatal conceit of traditional planning and zoning has led to these soulless suburbs. But aren't the conservatives substituting their own fatal conceit, that everyone wants to live in Small Town, USA?

Gordon: That's the weak link in the New Urbanism. If there were a grain of truth in their view, we would soon see people demanding it, and developers would strive to provide it. Builders are not ideologues.

New Urbanists say there are land use configurations that will lead to lower trip frequency. And if we object to the use of the automobile, then we can develop a land use solution. They have advanced all kinds of street designs, and hypothesized how to lay out homes and neighborhoods more compactly, and say if people can walk to all the places they need to go, presto, there will be less automobile use. The smallest introspection will show that trip frequency isn't fixed.

The New Urbanists certainly haven't done their homework. They certainly don't look at the facts a lot, so I keep going back to the international comparison. We've all traveled, we've all seen suburbanization in other parts in the world. There's clearly a universal demand for and use of automobiles that's reflected in the data.

International studies, like those from the Organization of Economic Cooperation and Development, are always funny to read, because the authors prejudge everything. At the beginning you have all these conclusions articulated that the automobile is the problem, what are we going to do with the automobile, how can we keep people out of automobiles, and so on. But what's revealing is that the authors lament automobile use in all these places. You have a tough time blaming American policy for automobile use [in other countries], and when you get rid of that explanation, you have to end up saying the reason people drive is consumer preference. Preference is a pretty powerful explanation compared to the one suggested by the New Urbanism.

Not just that, but the New Urbanists claim suburban development, which they call "sprawl," is something that people are using against their better judgment. One of the favorite themes of planners is that people haven't got enough choices, and builders are restricted by zoning codes to give people stuff that they don't really want. That's of course inconsistent with the other story the New Urbanists tell: that planners are beholden to builders. Well, if that's true, and just one of these greedy builders would figure out that people wanted to live in neotraditional settlements, then that greedy builder would overcome political barriers and we'd have the neotraditional developments.

Reason: Aren't there private attempts to create the type of places the New Urbanists want?

Gordon: I don't know of a lot of success stories. A lot of these developments are too new to judge. A lot of attention has been paid to the Disney-built community in Florida [Celebration], but the reviews of it have been mixed. Even that refers more to opinions of reviewers and less to the judgment of the market.

> *Traditional cities are fun for tourists. [That has] nothing to do with whether you want to live there.*

Reason: The New York Times Magazine has suggested it's more like living in a Disney-built theme park than in a real community.

Gordon: But social arrangements that are provided in the marketplace are constantly evolving. We would expect that savvy builders are evolving and experimenting in providing new things. It's a wonderful process.

If the New Urbanists have something to contribute to that evolution, that's wonderful. But instead they want to make a clean break and say that society is marching one way and we know the way it ought to go instead.

Reason: What's good about suburban living?

Gordon: Those of us who believe in markets place a lot of value on living arrangements that are an expression of consumer preferences. People are voting for spacious living, so by all means let them have what they are voting for. They're voting for access to their schools, they are voting for clean air and those kinds of things. By any measure, suburban living has to be a success story.

Americans run to [visit] Europe because, hell, those are cities. Now, that doesn't mean we choose to live there; it's just a nice place to visit. Traditional cities are fun for tourists. [That has] nothing to do with whether you want to live there.

There is the presumption that suburbanites are living these lives of quiet desperation and isolation, and they really hate being there. You see trotted out ideas about community being missing. And to have community, you've got to be in Manhattan. There are a lot of ex-Manhattanites that would challenge that theory very seriously.

Reason: A lot of people seem to think that auto travel is heavily subsidized but mass transit isn't.

Gordon: Federal transit subsidies go back to the 1960s, and for the first 10 years they were capital subsidies only. You had all this overbuilding of rail transit and a lot of people wrote articles that said overbuilding occurred because the feds subsidize only one part of the activity, and that's building. In 1974 the feds began subsidizing operation as well as building of transit systems. The whole idea of a federal transit policy may be silly, but as long as all this money is funneled though Washington, locals want to get in line to get theirs.

Whether you [do] it per mile or per trip, transit subsidies are hugely greater than any subsidies to the automobile. Per passenger mile, transit subsidies are 50 times what auto subsidies are. And the L.A. experience suggests that we spend a lot of money and get less transit use. We're spending more to get rid of riders. Back-of-the-envelope calculations show that about $7 billion has been spent on rail so far, and we know that they've lost an aggregate of about 1 billion riders over a 10-year span. So they've spent $7.00 for every transit rider eliminated.

Reason: How does that loss of ridership compare to the national average?

Gordon: There have been market-share losses in all of the new rail cities. The other thing you want to control for is background growth. So this is over a period where L.A. County added 12 percent to the population, and a lot of those were lower-skilled immigrants, who are sort of a natural constituency for mass transit. So to spend that much money and lose that many riders, that's not simple. You've really got to work at it.

Reason: Is any public transportation economically viable?

Gordon: At best, a maybe if you legalized vans. There's a big fight in New York City over them right now. Los Angeles legalized airport vans, and now Super Shuttle wants to get in the way of new entrants. But whatever [form of public transit] you come up with would be running neck and neck with large numbers of used cars. The transportation mode of choice of low-income people is used cars.

Reason: The communities that are held out as almost utopian by the New Urbanists—Portland, Oregon, or the Kentlands in suburban D.C.—have intensely politicized almost every private land use decision. Is putting every decision about painting your roof before a plebiscite the way people really want to live?

Gordon: That scares off a lot of people because they fear that their own property rights are up for grabs. If their own property rights are subject to being put in a common pool, a lot of people will say, "No, thank you."

On the other side, we have the growth of community associations, or what some people are calling entrepreneurial communities. When everything is contractual, then you're not going to have these surprises. So people are making ever more such choices, and it puts them in the category of getting out of harm's way and providing insurance for my property rights, because my property rights are ever more up for grabs, [depending upon what] judges are doing or not doing, or what the zoning board is doing in response to organized groups, and all that. The entrepreneurial communities—or whatever you want to call them, community associations—are a mechanism that fits very well.

> ## *The best thing that's happening to old urban cores is the immigrants.*

Reason: But can't community associations become political organizations that have as much power as zoning boards?

Gordon: If everything is covered by contract, there are no misunderstandings and no surprises. We either bargain for the contract that we want or we go look for another one somewhere else.

Reason: But contracts can't anticipate everything. An entrepreneurial community established 20 years ago could have never anticipated the development of 18-inch satellite dishes, which might well be banned in such a place.

Gordon: More adaptive forms will have to come on the market. My friend Spencer MacCallum, an anthropologist who writes on these issues, says that we may see the development of leasehold arrangements rather than traditional contract arrangements. The model he uses is that of hotels and shopping malls, where entrepreneurs provide services that people want. Leaseholds may provide much more flexible property arrangements than we typically imagine.

Reason: You mean the neighborhood association may renegotiate parts of its contract every year? We won't let you build a deck on the back of your house this year, but next year we'll think about it? Or people could decide to live in rigidly defined communities with extremely inflexible contracts if there's a demand for them?

Gordon: Right. All in the direction of increasing competition. People are more mobile than ever, and they have an easier time moving from one place to another as their requirements change.

The downside of these entrepreneurial communities, of course, is that as more affluent people withdraw from cities the interest groups that are left behind become ever more powerful. The people who are victims are the people who are least likely to move. We condemn the poorest to the worst public schools and the worst public services.

Reason: So are decaying urban cores part of an evolutionary process that no planning can overcome?

Gordon: The best thing that's happening to old urban cores is the immigrants, and immigrants have almost nothing to do with the planners except for the fact that planners often give them a hard time when they want to get occupational licenses. The infusion of capital and entrepreneurial skills in the core areas is coming entirely from the immigrants. If we make it our business to chase them out, then we may be hastening the decay of those urban cores.

Reason: You don't fit the profile of the typical urban planner, advocating top-down remedies. How did you arrive where you are? Are you indeed atypical?

Gordon: Planning is so eclectic it draws people from everywhere: architecture, the social sciences, the natural sciences. You really get an odd stew. I have a very Hayekian view of the world, and given the way that I view the evolution of the built environment, the Hayekian view has a lot to say. I teach about markets, so I'm less suspicious of market mechanisms than most of my planning colleagues.

And even when I speak with like-minded colleagues, I have to ask if market-friendly planning is realistic or plausible. Is there any mileage in doing market-friendly planning, or are spontaneous orders or spontaneous adjustments going to outdistance what planners try to do all the time? And that's why it's interesting to look at the migrations that are going on into the exurbs and into private communities, because those are going on in spite of any planning or any policy.

If we have local policy interests, and we have an understanding of the role of markets, then I think you reach the conclusion that a lot of the conventional, command-and-control stuff is disastrous. Spending $7.00 per rider to lose a billion transit riders is disastrous. So I think we have a huge case study which does not offer us any cause for optimism for traditional planning.

What can we, as researchers, really do? We can quit, or we can keep believing—let's unearth some of these facts and ideas, present them as best we can, and maybe somebody will learn something.

Reason: How are you perceived in the planning community? Are you on the fringe?

Gordon: I'm at the edge of the fringe.

Reason: So when you go to the American Planning Association's convention, do you drink alone?

Gordon: Well, I don't go very often. When I'm invited to speak at certain places, I think it's as a curiosity. There's the usual handful of people who thank you. God knows if they thank you because they've been informed or entertained or whatever.

But the intent is to uncover some facts, support them as best you can, put them in context, because there are all sorts of unfounded assertions out there.

Reason: Even so, the traditional planning community doesn't seem to shun you completely. In the Winter 1997 issue of the *American Planning Association Journal*, you and your USC colleague Harry Richardson engaged in a fascinating debate with Florida International University planning professor Reid Ewing. Your article, "Are Compact Cities a Desirable Goal?," was a straightforward exposition of the case against traditional planning and for consumer preferences. Ewing's "Is Los Angeles-Style Sprawl Desirable?" directly challenged your arguments. How did that come about?

Gordon: We sent them our article, and they wrote back and said, "We can run this if we run it with a counterpoint." There wasn't even the suggestion that they would run ours alone. I'm happy they did run both, because I want that discussion to be out there. Nevertheless, the editors of the journal of the APA felt they needed the safety of a counterpoint before even letting us present our side. But Harry and I were pleased to find out that the editors awarded us honorable mention for feature article of the year.

I was asked to address the L.A. City Planning Commission two years ago because there was a draft of their plan which favored transit-oriented development. And I said, "Here are the various reasons why it will not work." The response I got was a big yawn. There was zero interest in that, either [from] the commissioners who for some reason invited me, or [from] a lot of the staff people who were there. I just said their document was full of holes, but there was no interest as to asking why, or can you tell us what's wrong, or anything like that.

Reason: Is traditional planning becoming inconsequential? Are today's academic planners comparable to the slide-rule designers of 20 years ago, preparing to offer a product which has no market?

Gordon: We are trending away from planners in the traditional form, who primarily serve the interests of municipalities. But property arrangements are coming on line which require the developer to wear the planner's hat or the planner to wear the developer's hat. You could call this role "planning," but it's not traditional or public-sector planning.

People who are savvy enough to see the opportunities may be called planners, but they are less likely to operate in city hall and are more likely to operate in a development group, to arrange the types of developments that are successful. They will need a more sophisticated range of skills.

Maybe the world is changing so fast that what's coming out of the academy will lag behind [what the real world demands]. Maybe students will come out of the academy being trained in one way and find, once they leave, they need skills that direct them in another.

But that may be true of any number of other disciplines. It may be a problem professional schools in general face. We know universities are having a hard time keeping up. That's why we have think tanks [laughs].

Portland's Green Peace: At Play in the Fields of Urban Planning[4]

By Jay Walljasper
The Nation, October 13, 1997

Oregon has long attracted visitors seeking spectacular natural beauty—mountain peaks rising above the clouds, green cathedrals of spruce and fir, a wild seacoast dotted with rugged cliffs. But in recent years Oregon has also become known for its urban scenery. Town planners, city officials, environmentalists and neighborhood activists from all over the country are drawn to Portland to see sights like these:

- Tom McCall Park, a pleasant patch of green downtown—where kids splash in a fountain and couples walk hand in hand along the Willamette River—that was once the site of a freeway;

- downtown Portland itself, written off for dead thirty years ago, which now features block after block of lively storefronts, coffeehouses, restaurants, parks, rehabbed warehouses and office towers, plus a Chinatown and Powell's, the largest bookstore in America. The number of jobs downtown has doubled since 1971 with no net increase in parking spots, thanks to a popular light-rail line and efficient bus service;

- Martin Luther King Jr. Boulevard, which boasts new housing, stores and jobs along with dropping crime rates in the center of what has long been Portland's African-American ghetto;

- West Union Road, a two-lane blacktop 13 miles from downtown. On one side stand clusters of houses and apartment buildings, with swingsets and grills. Across the road lie rolling pastures and leafy orchards with only an occasional farmhouse. West Union Road marks Portland's Urban Growth Boundary, a line beyond which suburban development cannot sprawl;

- downtown Gresham, which sits just a few blocks from one end of the East Side light-rail line in this largely blue-collar suburb. The sidewalks now bustle with folks stopping at the new shops, new health club, new brew pub, new townhouses and a farmers' market. When another light-rail line opens on the West Side next year, passengers will be able to step out into several newly constructed downtowns. Beaverton, once a standard-issue sixties suburb, will host a town center with substantial housing, shopping and services around the train station. "You will no

---

4. "Portland's Green Peace" by Jay Walljasper. Reprinted with permission from the October 13, 1997, issue of *The Nation*.

longer be able to say there's no there there," boasts Beaverton mayor Rob Drake.

Portland attracts this interest from around the country because instead of accepting ever-escalating levels of traffic, air pollution, sprawl and inner-city decay, it offers a different version of what American cities could look like in the twenty-first century. Most other growing metropolitan regions, from Orlando to Minneapolis-St. Paul to Las Vegas, still follow in the tire tracks of Los Angeles, the classic twentieth-century city founded upon an unwavering commitment to freeways and new subdivisions. Since the sixties, however, Oregonians have looked south with horror. They didn't want to see their beloved forests, farms and foothills plowed under by spreading suburbs. Yet it was clear that Portland, with its scenic setting and mild temperatures, was going to grow. So discussion began about how urban growth could be managed to prevent the environmental and social problems afflicting other regions.

[Orego- nians] didn't want to see their beloved forests, farms and foothills plowed under by spreading suburbs.

The city took a first step toward a new kind of urban development in 1975 when Mayor Neil Goldschmidt (later Secretary of Transportation in the Carter Administration), responding to intense pressure from community groups in working-class Southeast Portland, canceled plans for the Mount Hood freeway, which would have ripped apart several neighborhoods to accommodate suburban commuters. The East Side light-rail line was later built to replace the freeway.

The cause of growth management won another major victory the next year when environmentalists teamed up with maverick Republican governor Tom McCall to enact an ambitious statewide program of land-use planning that required all cities, including Portland, to establish an Urban Growth Boundary. Conservatives, timber companies and real estate developers fiercely opposed it, but the measure gained wide support from the general public, who saw it as the only way to prevent Oregon from being overrun by Southern California-style sprawl.

In another significant move, Portland area voters in 1979 approved plans to establish an elected regional government, Metro, which is still the only one in the country. Although this initiative was promoted by "good government" advocates rather than grassroots activists, Metro has proved very effective in administrating growth-management policies. Efforts to limit sprawl in other regions have been hampered by the clashing self-interests of various municipal, county and state authorities.

Two decades later the wisdom of these decisions is borne out by Portland's attractiveness as a place to live. Since 1991 there have been few violations of clean-air guidelines for auto emissions, whereas in the seventies Portland missed the mark almost one day out of three. Eight hundred and fifty million dollars in new development has gone up along the light-rail lines, and Portland ranks number one among medium-sized U.S. cities in transit use. Sixty-five percent of all riders own cars, notes G. B. Arrington, director of strategic planning for the local transit authority: "This is not a system just for the poor, the elderly and people with D.W.I.s."

Portland has not eliminated sprawl—you still see plenty of strip malls and subdivisions—but the city has contained it. Suburbia stops on all sides of the city between three to eighteen miles from downtown, giving way to fields and forests. The average lot size of new single-family houses has dropped from about 10,000 square feet in 1979 to about 7,000 last year. Metro officials are planning for 600,000 new residents in the next forty years but plan to add as much as 18,600 acres of new land to the Urban Growth Boundary—a 40 percent increase in population being accommodated with only 8 percent growth in area. (By contrast, the Detroit metropolitan region has increased 0.3 percent in population over the past two decades, but expanded in size by 18 percent.) This means that most new housing, shopping and workplaces will be built in existing communities, including the inner city.

John Fregonese, Metro's director of growth-management services, notes that the municipality of Portland granted permits for 2,600 new units of housing last year in a city that is already built up. This is happening on top of an explosion of refurbishing old houses and revitalizing neighborhood business districts. Some Portland neighborhoods are beginning to approach what residents of New York or Toronto would consider a real city: a place where you can easily walk to grocery stores, drugstores, cafes, parks, child care centers and specialty stores. "The Urban Growth Boundary bounces investment back inward," says Henry Richmond, co-founder of the environmental group 1,000 Friends of Oregon. "The older suburbs get more investment and so does the inner city. Europe's done this for a century. That's why its cities look the way they do."

Myron Orfield, a Minnesota state legislator gaining national recognition for his ideas about how to save inner-city neighborhoods and blue-collar suburbs, points to Portland as the leader in urban revitalization efforts. "It isn't perfect," he says, "but it's better than anywhere else in the country." Orfield offers a few suggestions on how Portland could do a better job of insuring its overall vitality: sharing of property tax revenues between wealthy and needy municipalities and enacting "fair share" housing measures, which halt exclusionary zoning that keeps low- and middle-income households out of upscale communities. Fair share housing regulations are currently being promoted in Portland by a coalition of environmental and social justice groups.

Grass-roots activism has also become a permanent fixture in Portland's political picture over the past twenty-five years. In the early nineties, for example, a proposed freeway expansion on the city's West Side, which met little opposition from elected officials, was stopped dead by residents who enlisted the help of 1,000 Friends of Oregon. Using sophisticated planning studies, freeway opponents proved to state officials that light rail and smart land-use planning could meet the area's future transportation needs.

Right now, 1,000 Friends is busy suing Metro over the recent decision to add farmland to the urban growth reserve over the next four decades. While acknowledging the need to add perhaps a few thousand acres, 1,000 Friends director Robert Liberty says 18,000 is too many and sends developers the message that they don't really have to change much about the way they build houses, malls and office projects. Many home builders and real estate interests have long opposed Portland's growth-management policies, and they financed ballot referendum campaigns to repeal the state land-use laws in 1976, 1978 and 1982; 1,000 Friends rallied voters to beat back all three attempts and continues to campaign against efforts in the Republican-dominated state legislature to make land-use planning more laissez-faire. State laws bolster Portland's growth-management policies by making it harder for developers to leapfrog the city's growth boundary and start constructing the usual sprawl in outlying areas. Growth management activists are also gearing up for a possible statewide ballot initiative next year to abolish Metro, which is being proposed by an influential antitax gadfly who condemns the agency as an unnecessary layer of government.

In their fight to preserve growth-management policies, 1,000 Friends and other environmental groups can call on some unexpected allies: the conservative Oregon Farm Bureau, which wants to protect farmland; suburban mayors, who understand that if development keeps moving out to the fringes their towns are next in line for urban decline; and a growing number of developers, who've figured out there's still lots of money to be made building more compact projects inside the Urban Growth Boundary. But opponents of strict growth-management policies are formidable. Don Morissette, a house builder who spent a small fortune to get himself elected to the Metro council, argues, "There is very little undeveloped land inside the current U.G.B. Adding 248,000 households and 460,000 jobs over the next 20 years will radically change neighborhoods and our quality of life." He helped to lead the charge at Metro to get the 18,000 more acres added to the growth boundary when environmentalists wanted a smaller or no expansion. The big question fight now is how much of those 18,000 acres will be opened for development in the near future.

But even Morissette acknowledges, "The boundary has been good for this region." While battles still rage over where to draw the line on sprawl, virtually no one wants the kind of unbridled suburban development they see elsewhere. Public support for the growth boundary remains high (it was favored nearly 3-to-1 in a recent survey conducted by Metro), although many people share Morissette's concern about what the higher-density development necessary to prevent sprawl will mean. (Another Metro survey shows that a plurality of respondents would accept more density in their neighborhoods over expansions of the growth boundary.)

"I'm convinced people aren't really afraid of density. They're afraid of bad design," says Marcy McInelly, an architect and urban activist. "Some of the classic neighborhoods in Portland that everyone loves are designed for density. But when people hear of density, they think of high-rise housing projects."

When Portland began its growth-management strategy two decades ago, local and national opponents said it would choke the region's economic prosperity. Since the city is booming, critics have shifted gears and now contend that growth management hurts poor and middle-income people by driving up the cost of living. *Forbes* made that case in an article published this past spring, quoting a report from the National Association of Home Builders that said Portland was "second only to San Francisco in the unaffordability of its housing, in terms of local income."

Affordable housing advocate Tasha Harmon disputes these conclusions. She points out that land, generally one-quarter the total price of housing, is the only cost affected by the Urban Growth Boundary, and that the 60 percent rise in Portland's land prices is

---

"People aren't really afraid of density. They're afraid of bad design."—Marcy McInelly, architect and urban activist

---

less than that of many other fast-growing areas that don't have growth boundaries, including Salt Lake City (76 percent), Houston (79 percent) and Chattanooga (134 percent). Growth management may be responsible for rising housing costs only to the extent that it has made Portland a desirable place to live, attracting thousands of newcomers who fuel the real estate boom.

What is a problem in Portland, Harmon says, is gentrification. All the new development in inner-city neighborhoods displaces people living there. Low-income people who own their homes or have the skills to take advantage of jobs being created downtown or along the light-rail lines benefit from revitalization. But others find themselves paying steeper rent, searching for cheaper housing or living on the streets. "Gentrification is a mixed bag," Harmon says. "But the hollowing out of our cities is hard on poor people, too. Growth management has the potential to make life better in the inner city. But it doesn't happen automatically."

That's where the Coalition for a Livable Future comes in. Harmon's group, the Community Development Network, is one of thirty-eight local organizations, ranging from the Audubon Society to the Urban League, that have joined forces to promote growth management but also to make sure that the benefits extend to low-

and middle-income people. Zack Semke, who coordinates the coalition out of the offices of 1,000 Friends of Oregon, notes, "It's a simple but powerful fact that the faster the rate of sprawl, the faster the rate of disinvestment in the inner city." The coalition emphasizes the link between issues like land use, affordable housing, economic opportunity, green spaces, sustainable transportation and neighborhood vitality. "It's an astonishing coalition," enthuses Harmon. "The conservatives can't do a divide-and-conquer strategy—getting the social justice advocates against the environmentalists."

This is not to say that Portland offers a miracle cure for all that ails our cities. Ron Herndon, an African-American neighborhood activist, notes that improved public schools and better job training programs are more critical to helping low-income communities than an Urban Growth Boundary and light-rail transit. And Lenny Dee, an activist working with the coalition, adds that moneyed interests can still bend the rules to get what they want, such as a new downtown parking ramp built in what was supposed to be a pedestrian-oriented zone near the light-rail line.

Nonetheless, what's happening in Portland represents a new dimension in urban politics: adding concerns about social equity to the issues of environmental quality in the debate over how our cities should develop. The case for spending money to revitalize poor neighborhoods is strengthened by arguments about protecting green spaces on the edge of town, and vice versa. Middle-class people's worries about the livability of their neighborhoods are tied to broader issues of economic opportunity, sustainable transportation, compact development and affordable housing. Activists in Portland have successfully spread the message that our current pattern of urban growth—sprawling new development at the fringes and decay spreading out from the center—is too costly for both society and the environment.

"Most people here believe we shouldn't leave anything as important as how our cities grow to the private sector," explains Robert Liberty, adding that there's no reason this idea couldn't be embraced in other metropolitan areas. "The explanations people give for why Portland is different are hogwash. It's not the scenery. What sets us apart is our attitude toward growth management. And the reason we've accomplished what we've accomplished is that we've been working on it hard for 25 years."

Anti-Box Rebellion[5]

By Jonathan Walters
Governing, July 2000

Like thousands of places around the country, the town of Hat-field, Massachusetts, has always taken a rather casual approach toward controlling commercial development. Which is to say, it barely controls it at all. Certain parts of the town are zoned commercial. There are some general, minimal standards by which to review projects. But beyond that, it's strictly a hands-off policy. For the most part, developers make the big decisions on use, size and building design. Nor is there any evaluation of a project's potential economic effect. Whatever fiscal impact might come—good or bad—is just treated as a roll of the dice. Hatfield, in other words, is a big-box retailer's kind of town.

In fact, it might be regarded as a big-box retailer's dream come true. Situated above an easy bend in the Connecticut River just north of the bustling college town of Northampton, and connected umbilically to Interstate 91, Hatfield easily could have attracted one or more big-box companies a long time ago. But it was only last year that Home Depot began casing the neighborhood, looking for a spot to drop another stadium-sized store with miles-of-aisles of bargain building materials. It was a wake-up call.

Or, perhaps it would be better to say a pre-wake-up call. Home Depot didn't purchase any land or file an application to build anything. It just came on a scouting trip.

But that scouting trip was the reason this year's Hatfield town meeting—held over the course of two nights in May—evolved into an interesting exercise in the civics of growth management. On the docket were two measures, referred to by initiates simply as Article 28 and Article 30. Nondescript, perhaps, but to supporters—sitting in folding aluminum chairs on the high school gymnasium floor—those two bits of business represented a chance to build a firewall between the town's laissez-faire development attitude and an invasion of what critics refer to derisively as "sprawl marts." To the other side, of course, the measures represented something entirely different—an unwelcome step toward meddlesome municipal land use regulation.

First up was item 28, a one-year moratorium on all retail development over 10,000 square feet, which would give the town time to update its master plan. Item 30, the companion measure, would amend the town's zoning law to allow for a much more thorough review of all major retail development in the future to determine its impact on Hatfield. With each measure requiring a two-thirds majority to pass, supporters were predicting close votes. And so, as the town meeting worked its way through early items of business—anteing up $23,000 for painting and repairs to the town hall, paying $165,000 into the retirement system—the answer to a simple but central question loomed closer in Hatfield: Was a small New England town going to seize control of its own development destiny, or continue to leave it all up to circumstance and whoever happened to come along with a commercial proposition?

It is a question that more and more communities are beginning to wrestle with. Indeed, the fight over land use regulation in Hatfield represents a new front in the battle of the big-box store. In the past, the typical fight against one of these stores—which critics excoriate for their pave-it-over approach to design and their predatory effect on local small business—has been a last-ditch effort pulled together by volunteers, many of whom were never civically active before. Such fights typically begin after the decision is all but made. Realtors, developers and retailers have scouted the terrain, zeroed in on a site, lined up powerful local allies and legal assistance, and

---

The new approach is very simple: Be ready for mega-retailers such as Home Depot, Costco, Target and Wal-Mart before they come to town.

---

started drawing specific plans to move in. It's no surprise when such opposition fails.

The new approach is very simple: Be ready for mega-retailers such as Home Depot, Costco, Target and Wal-Mart before they come to town. Communities around the country are finding a wide assortment of ways to do this. In some places, they are rewriting design guidelines to blunt the physical impact of superstores (for example, by requiring that parking be hidden behind buildings or that the structures themselves come closer to sidewalks). Or they are using land use laws to steer development away from open space and back downtown—or at least into existing empty malls or large buildings.

Elsewhere, developers are being asked to provide a detailed independent study of the impact a giant retailer would have on property values, local merchants, the cost of emergency services and overall tax rates. Localities can use the results of such studies to ask for modification of a project, or to reject the development outright.

At the same time, some localities are asking the larger question of whether they need any more retail development at all. A number of them are taking a hard look at the ratio of commercial development to population in order to guard against retail overbuilding. If they decide that they are already overbuilt, they may oppose any new projects, big-box or otherwise. Or, if they are bold enough, they can take the ultimate step: simply zone big developments out of town by placing a cap on the size of any new retail facility.

No matter which strategy a community uses, in the end it usually comes down to zoning codes. In the words of Al Norman, the Greenfield, Massachusetts, resident who has been fighting big-box stores for a decade, "There is no single word in the developer's lexicon that is so hated as the six-letter word 'zoning.'"

One of the first communities to act preemptively on the big-box issue was Fort Collins, Colorado, which had already witnessed downtown devastation in the 1970s, when it lost Sears, Walgreens, J.C. Penney and Montgomery Ward to mall development on the fringes of town. When Fort Collins saw big-box stores circling to land in the early 1990s, it passed a six-month development moratorium, then used that time to beef up its design-review criteria for any retail development of more than 25,000 square feet. As a result, Fort Collins became a pioneer in requiring big-boxers to pay attention to facade design, building materials and colors, and the placement of parking, sidewalks and entrances. The city recently used this approach to soften the impact of a 200,000-square-foot Wal-Mart that is beginning construction this summer.

Fort Collins didn't ban the project outright, because it no longer feels any need to do that: The city's downtown has returned to life as a thriving boutique, restaurant and specialty-store center, and isn't really threatened by superstores. But the city does want considerably more control over what comes in and how it's built.

Even that sort of regulation rarely sits well with companies that are used to their own formula for putting in stores. One of the most contentious items surrounding the Wal-Mart project in Fort Collins, for example, was the city's requirement that the developer drastically scale back parking in front of the building. "They didn't like doing it," says chief planner Ted Shepard. "They fought us." But the city stuck to its guns, and the resulting agreement made it clear that in Fort Collins, at least, the sea-of-asphalt-in-front-of-pre-fab-corrugated-metal-monolith era was drawing to a close.

Vermont, famous among sprawl opponents for being the last state in the union to hold out against Wal-Mart, has seen its towns move on to a strategy of allowing the retail giant in, but forcing it to go where the community wants—not just anyplace Wal-Mart feels like going. In Bennington, in the southwest part of the state, the company was steered into a dead mall on the outskirts of town. Perhaps not an ideal location from a downtown-revival standpoint but still within what Bennington calls its "urban envelope." In Rutland, to the north, Wal-Mart agreed to go into an available space right in the town center.

But for some communities, neither the Fort Collins nor the Vermont strategy is tough enough. They want to keep the big-boxes out altogether. And some are finding ways of doing that.

In St. Petersburg, Florida, where Wal-Mart wanted to drop in a 220,000-square-foot "supercenter"—the size of four football fields—planning staff successfully argued that the project would exacerbate the city's already out-of-whack population-to-commercial-land ratio. According to the St. Petersburg Comprehensive Plan, an "oversupply" of retail space exists when there is more than one acre of commercial land for every 150 residents. An analysis done two years in advance of the Wal-Mart proposal found that the city was already at one acre of commercial land for every 143 residents. The project was rejected.

Conceivably, circumstances might change in St. Petersburg and such a project would be allowed in. Which is why the ultimate inoculation against big-box development is more straightforward: Amend your zoning code's schedule of dimensions—that all-important table usually tucked into the back of the ordinance that lists the height, size and setback requirements for various types of development.

This past March, the town of Boxborough, Massachusetts, updated its commercial zoning schedule of dimensions to prohibit any retail structure larger than 25,000 square feet (the average big-box routinely breaks 100,000). In Boxborough, there will be no debates at all over the impact of a big-box; as long as the ordinance remains unchanged, they're never going to get one. "We had a Home Depot looking at the west side of town," says Scott Robinson, one of the local activists who helped engineer the cap. "We decided we didn't want 10,000 cars a day driving through our neighborhoods."

But it's not just the impact of stores on their own towns that some communities worry about; it's what happens in the next town over. While the long-term economic benefit of superstores is a subject of debate—some argue they ultimately cost a local government more than they bring in—the prospect of property tax and sales tax money associated with a new store often allows developers to play one jurisdiction off against another. If Ourtown says a superstore has to meet certain design standards, a developer can threaten to jump over the border to Theirtown if Ourtown officials don't capitulate.

When jurisdictions join forces, developers have considerably less leverage in their fight to make governments conform to the big-box blueprint. In Fort Collins, for example, there would be no benefit to Wal-Mart in jumping just over the town line onto unincorporated county property, even though the county places virtually no zoning restrictions at all on commercial development. That's because under an intergovernmental agreement that the city has with the county, any development immediately adjacent to Fort Collins is automatically annexed to the city.

Such intergovernmental cooperation is still rare, however, which makes Hatfield, Massachusetts, an even more interesting study in the new preemptive approach. The six-month moratorium that was debated in May was part of a deal worked out with nearby Northampton, and the deal was this: The site that was originally being considered by Home Depot—the one that inspired Hatfield to propose tighter land use controls—actually straddled the Hatfield/Northampton line. To gain the control it wanted, Hatfield not only had to amend its own law, it had to persuade Northampton not to allow development on its share of the parcel pending Hatfield's master plan and zoning code update. But Northampton, in turn, needed to be convinced that Hatfield wouldn't turn around and scoop up Home Depot all for itself if Northampton held off. The way to do that was for Hatfield to pass Article 28, the one-year moratorium.

So quite a bit was resting on the debate in the high school gym that warm evening in May. Not only the question of whether Hatfield would begin to exercise more control over development within its boundaries, but whether two jurisdictions would begin working cooperatively on land use plans that affected them both—or whether relations might deteriorate into damaging competition for development.

As Article 28 finally made its way to the floor, the relatively brisk pace of the meeting ground to a crawl. For an hour, residents argued back and forth about the merits and the potential impact of the moratorium. Opponents said that it was flat-out antibusiness and anti-landowner. Some added that Northampton couldn't be trusted to keep up its end of the zoning bargain and that as soon as Hatfield passed its moratorium, Northampton would rezone those abutting parcels and start recruiting retail development that might have been Hatfield's. The other side insisted that the moratorium created vital breathing room to work on the master plan and to think through a host of issues around zoning and land use planning for the 21st century. Defeat of the moratorium, this faction said, might incite a pointless and divisive retail recruitment competition just as the two towns were taking the first tentative steps toward working together.

In the end, the vote proved to be no contest. Residents approved the moratorium 128 to 23. Then, the next night, the town meeting approved Article 30, the zoning amendment calling for more detailed scrutiny of all retail development of more than 10,000 square feet. It passed by an even more resounding 119 to 3.

Articles 28 and 30 are relatively modest measures when compared with what other towns and cities have been doing on land use. Yet it was hard to avoid the feeling in listening to the debates and then witnessing the votes that citizens of a small community had just spoken out loudly and clearly about who would be calling the development shots in town from then on. They would.

Turning Edge Cities Into Real Cities[6]

BY JONATHAN BARNETT
PLANNING, NOVEMBER 2002

Addison, Texas, began as a suburb on the northern edge of Dallas, then became part of "the Blade Runner Landscape" of gaudy buildings, vast parking lots, and huge signs along the North Dallas Tollway that Joel Garreau described in his 1991 book, *Edge Cities: Life on the New Frontier.*

His definition of an edge city is a relatively dry recital of statistics: 5,000,000 square feet of leasable office space; 600,000 square feet of retail space; a significant increase in daytime population on weekdays; and—most important—a location that was farmland or suburban residential neighborhood 30 to 40 years ago.

But Garreau is not just an observer; he is a partisan. His book begins: "The controversial assumption undergirding this book is that Americans basically are pretty smart cookies who generally know what they're doing." Garreau fully deserves the recognition he has received for his original and effective research, his ability to give a vivid name and definition to urban development in the suburbs and exurbs, and his superb abilities as a story teller. But what about his "controversial assumption"? Yes, Americans are smart cookies. But Garreau fails to allow for the possibility that the interaction of individual developers with outmoded zoning codes and single-minded highway designs could produce a result that is a lot less than smart.

Today part of Addison is being transformed into something much more like a real city: a place with streets and sidewalks, where street frontages have stores and restaurants on the ground floors, where the parking is tucked away in garages, and the offices and apartment buildings define spaces along the street, or around landscaped urban squares and hidden courtyards. The North Dallas Tollway is still the front door, but the city is also planning development to take advantage of a future stop on a new crosstown rapid transit line.

Farther out the North Dallas Tollway in Plano, the Legacy Town Center is taking shape in the middle of a 2,600-acre development of corporate office buildings isolated from each other on large landscaped estates. As in Addison, the Legacy Town Center is planned as a network of urban streets and sidewalks, with buildings defining the space of the streets and squares, and with the parking along the street or in garages supporting a mix of offices, a hotel, apartments, and retail.

The first quadrant of development is built around a park with an ornamental lake. An easy walk of a few blocks leads to a village of retail streets near the exit from the tollway. The heavily secured front gate of the EDS corporate headquarters is also within walking distance of the Legacy park and lake, although right now the walk is through open, undeveloped land.

In both Addison and the Legacy Town Center a key component is a five-story elevator apartment building that, along with the streetfront retail and garage parking, produces a true urban lifestyle. There turns out to be a market for urban living in these edge locations, the same kind of interest in having a home within walking distance of shops and entertainment that is also helping to re-energize traditional city centers.

The developments at Addison and Legacy were begun by Columbus Realty Trust, later acquired by Post Properties; in both cases RTKL was the urban designer. Addison saw its position as the prime edge city in Dallas's favored quarter challenged by development farther out in Plano. And in Plano, the owners of Legacy found that their office tenants were looking for places to have lunch, to shop on the way home, and to live closer to their workplace. Both turned to a more traditional kind of urbanism to give themselves a competitive advantage.

The city of Addison took on the cost of the public environment in the Addison Circle district, and the owners of Legacy sought development that would make Legacy more than just a corporate office park. It will be a long time, if ever, before rapid transit reaches Plano, a city that does not participate in the Dallas Area Rapid Transit system. But should there be a change in policy, there is one part of Plano that will be a compact, walkable, mixed-used community, capable of being served by transit. When the DART crosstown line is built, Addison will also be ready; the station will be located at the center of a district planned to receive it.

Past Trends Are Not Predestination

Most of the edge cities that Garreau documented could only be reached by car. Single-use buildings isolated amid wide expanses of parking also made a car necessary to go to lunch or to the building next door; there were few public spaces and public amenities. It did not seem likely that such places might evolve into compact, walkable, mixed-use communities with parks and tree-lined streets, and—of course—such a transformation is still unusual.

Robert E. Lang of the Fannie Mae Foundation, writing approximately a decade after Garreau, has identified another phenomenon that he calls Edgeless Cities. Lang's research indicates that a majority of new suburban office space is not going into places that meet Garreau's definition of an edge city, but into a much more diffuse pattern of commercial corridors and isolated office parks that are spread out over hundreds of square miles and are not recognized by the public as being part of a single destination.

Lang does not believe this kind of development is likely to coalesce into any kind of city. He sees it as a defensive response to traffic congestion, and a symptom of the continuing rapid advance of sprawl.

The vitality and rapid growth of both edge cities and edgeless urbanization has impressed other observers as the inevitable result of powerful market forces, notably architect and avant-garde theorist Rem Koolhaas, who included wonderstruck descriptions about highway-oriented development in his recent compendium, *S, M, L, XL*. Here is the future, he says, like it or not.

Garreau was correct that few in the planning profession understood the edge city phenomenon until it was already well advanced; and he makes it clear that many developers did not understand what they were helping to produce until they could actually see what they and their competitors had built. But once planners grasped the scale of what has been happening, and once developers understood that they were helping to create new cities, the shapeless edge city has been shown to be far from inevitable.

The vitality and rapid growth of both edge cities and edgeless urbanization has impressed observers as the inevitable result of powerful market forces.

Channeling New Development Forces

One of the first prototypes for channeling these new development forces was built in downtown Boca Raton, Florida, where the city acquired a failed two-department-store mall along a highway and made the site available to developers. The development that replaces the mall, Mizner Park, designed by Richard Heapes, then at Cooper, Carry architects, is built around a new main street, a wide boulevard running parallel to U.S. Highway 1. Arcaded shops line this street on both sides. There are offices over the retail on the side nearest to U.S. 1 and a successful apartment development over and behind the stores on the quieter, more residential side. All the parking is in garages, except for a few on-street spaces.

The next street over, wide and landscaped, is the edge of single-family residential neighborhood. Mizner Park's garages on that side are lined with narrow townhouses, in scale with the houses across the street. The use of such "liner buildings" is an important technique for creating lively streets and for integrating new high-density development into lower-density surroundings.

Within its boundaries, Mizner Park is a true urban place. Yes, its grand boulevard terminates in the parking lots and stores of the strip-mall next door, but this anticlimax also implies that the design of Mizner Park could be extended for many more urban blocks.

RTKL and Sasaki's design for the Reston Town Center in northern Virginia is also a significant prototype. Reston—the name stands for Robert E. Simon's town—was always a planned community; but when construction began in the early 1960s it was thought to be a satellite new town for Washington, D.C. No one predicted that it would be part of a corridor of high-density development extending from Tysons Corner out to Dulles airport.

Today the Reston Town Center is in some ways just another office park in the Dulles corridor, but it organizes its series of office buildings along a main street with shopping on the ground floor. There are movie theaters and a hotel, and an apartment tower at one end of the street. Other apartment and townhouse districts are developing within walking distance.

The Redmond Town Center, designed by LMN Architects for a site adjacent to downtown Redmond, Washington, is another interesting alternative to the single-use developments that have been the components of edge cities. A developer tried for 18 years to develop a conventional mall in this location. Today there is a street and block system connected to the existing downtown. There is a central retail plaza attached to a parking deck, and the rest of the site is developed as an office center, with streetfront retail, a hotel, and some additional retail buildings. The developer is currently adding a second hotel and the Town Center's first department store, attracted to the already established retail core—completely the reverse of the way conventional malls are developed, where nothing goes forward until the anchor department store tenants have been signed up.

Why the Real Estate Market Needs a New Model

People used to say that the typical edge city development constructed around highway interchanges works perfectly well and makes money for the owners, so how can it be criticized for not following a hypothetical better model?

The answer is that many of these highway-oriented developments are rapidly becoming a problem because they no longer make money for their owners. First-generation retail malls are failing. Their department stores have closed; some storefronts are empty, and others aren't paying any rent. New super-regional malls have opened in these markets, and the older malls can't compete with them.

The first generation of highway-oriented hotels have a hard time competing with newer and better hotels located in or near office parks that supply a steady stream of customers. Highway-oriented office buildings are nowhere near as attractive a working environment as offices in newer suburban office parks and so are partly vacant. Much development along the highway is not just a mess as urban design; it is a failure as real estate.

In 2000 the Congress for the New Urbanism sponsored a study by PriceWaterhouseCoopers of regional shopping malls. The study concluded that seven percent of these malls were older structures in poor competitive positions because of low rents and empty stores. The study characterized these malls as Greyfields. Another 12 percent are vulnerable, and could become Greyfields in the next few years. As they lose their original economic rational, these shopping malls can provide a key to retrofitting an edge city because of their large parking fields and accessible locations, frequently in one quadrant of a highway interchange.

Edge cities have a big reservoir of land devoted to at-grade parking for offices as well as for shopping. As land values increase, it becomes possible to decant some of this parking into garages, creating sites for new development. In many edge cities, existing zoning allows such additional development by right, as the initial structures are below zoning limits because of the constraints of at-grade parking.

The peak traffic pattern for high-density residential development mostly moves in the reverse direction from traffic generated by offices. Apartments are feasible in edge city locations where congestion on surrounding highways limits additional office development. The extensive amount of housing built recently at Tysons Corner in Fairfax County, Virginia, is an interesting indicator because Tysons is considered by many to be the proverbial edge city.

The Galleria District in Houston, one of the nation's oldest edge cities, has recently become a tax increment reinvestment zone. Property owners are taxing themselves to construct, retroactively, the streets and parking systems needed to support high-density development. The decision to take action was caused by competition from newer development on the rapidly expanding edge of the Houston metropolitan area. One feature of Uptown Houston's plans is a transitway along Post Oak Boulevard, which could connect to Houston's rapid transit system as it develops. A similar process of reinvention is taking place in Buckhead, a comparable uptown location in Atlanta that already has two stops on the regional rapid transit system.

Arlington County's Two Downtowns

When the Washington Metropolitan Transit System was being planned in the 1960s, Arlington County recognized the potential for the transit to support new development. Plans for one of the transit lines called for it to run through Arlington down the center of Route 66. The stations would be islands in the middle of the highway, having little influence on development in the areas immediately surrounding the stations.

The county was able to put together the additional financing to have the metro built in a tunnel that runs parallel to the highway about half a mile to the south, more or less along the route of Wilson Boulevard, a traditional commercial corridor. The tunnel rejoins the highway about halfway across Arlington County, and the line continues in the center of Route 66 out into Fairfax County. There are five stops in Arlington County: Rosslyn, Court House, Clarendon, Virginia Square, and Ballston.

> *The future dynamic for edge cities is to evolve into more traditional downtowns.*

This corridor was actually identified by Joel Garreau as an edge city, but it is very different from the automobile-based development pattern in most such suburban locations. Wilson Boulevard, with the adjacent Clarendon Boulevard, forms a one-way pair and continues to be a major traffic corridor. This area has been given a completely new structure by the transit system, particularly at Rosslyn and Ballston, at either end of the corridor, which have become very like traditional downtowns.

Pentagon City and Crystal City, also in Arlington County but on a different branch of the transit system, have also developed as concentrated urban districts. The Arlington County examples show what could happen in the next generation if rapid transit systems are added to commercial corridors that already have a high intensity of development.

Policy Implications

These early indications suggest that the future dynamic for edge cities is to evolve into more traditional downtowns, with a balanced mix of uses, including the potential to add enough residential development to become a "24-hour city" and enough density to support rapid transit as an adjunct, at least, to automobile access. Local governments that support these incipient trends with appropriate zoning and transportation policies are likely to accelerate the process.

In areas that are still developing, the highway connections that make edge cities possible have to be recognized for what they are, and the desirability of creating new edge city locations should be evaluated before a highway is built. There are still many new highway plans that could produce edge cities. Proposed outer beltways or ring roads to facilitate peripheral commuting multiply the potential for edge cities geometrically, as can be seen in the extraordinary dispersal of urban growth taking place in Houston.

If a particular highway connection is seen as a desirable location for an edge city, specific plans for the area should be created in advance. These plans should include configurations for the interchange and other highway connections that are compatible with future development. Local zoning has to become a template for a desirable future, and not just a vague set of instructions that will be interpreted only after a development is proposed. If a highway location is not considered appropriate for an edge city, planning policies should be followed to keep it from developing in this way—for example, by not extending the necessary water and sewer connections.

Putting more money into regional transit systems, and not just highways, would permit edge cities to become part of a transportation network, and would alleviate regional gridlock problems. At the same time, edge cities would have to become more dense and more walkable, so that they could be served effectively by transit.

Americans are basically pretty smart cookies, and, when they make a mistake, they can generally figure out how to fix it.

Poor Area Heart of Plan

Eyes Are Finally on Overtown[7]

BY NICOLE WHITE
THE MIAMI HERALD, APRIL 29, 2003

For years the residents of Overtown, Miami's poorest neighborhood, have waited for the tales of rebirth, redevelopment and revitalization to take life in their neighborhood.

Instead, each year they've watched with increasing despair as new development has turned other struggling neighborhoods into pockets of prosperity, somehow shunning this neighborhood that's been yearning for a chance to be what it once was: one of the most prosperous black neighborhoods in Miami.

Now two Cuban-American Republican lawmakers say they have the answer to Overtown's woes. Sen. Alex Diaz de la Portilla and freshman Rep. David Rivera are pushing legislation to create a tax-free urban revitalization zone to entice businesses to the area.

With only a week to go in the Legislature, the proposal faces an uphill battle because it was introduced too late. But supporters have vowed to bring it up again next year.

"Overtown is the poorest of the poor in Miami," said Rivera. "Everyone in Miami, regardless of race or party affiliation, should be embarrassed enough to do something."

But there are plenty of skeptics.

The fact that the proposal is being pushed by two Hispanic politicians, who represent constituencies that are ethnically and financially worlds apart from the realities of Overtown, has raised some eyebrows.

Is this, they ask, the manifestation of rumors that powerful business forces have spent years dreaming up ways to take over the neighborhood? There is not much land left to develop in the city. Overtown is just north of downtown Miami and, like much of the new redevelopment that's slowly transforming the city, it could one day be the perfect neighborhood for those in the business community tired of commuting to the suburbs. Or is Diaz de la Portilla helping Overtown because his brother Miguel Diaz de la Portilla may need the support of the black community as he runs for mayor next year?

Alex Diaz de la Portilla says his intentions are pure: "If the quality of life in one part of the county is hurting, then that's important to me."

7. Article by Nicole White from *The Miami Herald* April 29, 2003. Copyright © *The Miami Herald*. Reprinted with permission.

Diaz de la Portilla says his track record speaks for itself, because he's voted for empowerment zones in the past to help the blighted neighborhood.

As the second-highest-ranking senator, he says he now has a louder voice in the Legislature and can do more: "I'm doing this for people who cannot afford a lobbyist to care about their issue."

But longtime resident and activist Irby McKnight says while he thinks the idea is novel, he admits he's leery.

"Of course I have concerns," McKnight said.

McKnight said he was suspicious when Rivera first asked to meet with him to tour the neighborhood and then told him of his plans. But McKnight insists he will use his position as chairman of the Overtown Neighborhood Assembly as a "bully pulpit" to make sure the residents are not pushed aside.

Concerns Aside

For now, McKnight, who's heard a number of empty promises in the 33 years he's lived in the neighborhood, says he'll set aside his concerns because he thinks Rivera, irrespective of any political ambitions, may actually be sincere.

"He did his homework. He came to the neighborhood, unlike other people who stayed from afar" and decided that empowerment zones and redevelopment agencies are "what we should do to help," McKnight said.

The proposal is straightforward: New businesses would be exempt from paying or collecting sales taxes. The exemptions would be granted for 10 years and would also be extended to some existing businesses that qualify. To qualify, businesses would have to hire at least 20 percent of their workforce from the neighborhood.

A seven-member oversight board—to include an appointee by the governor, mayor and a resident—would screen applicants to avoid an influx of too-similar businesses and evaluate the program annually. The measure has the support of Miami mayor Manny Diaz and city manager Joe Arriola, who have both indicated a willingness to offer some property tax relief to businesses that qualify.

"We're excited to see that someone is sponsoring the legislation, and we are supportive," said Javier Fernandez, a senior assistant to Arriola.

Overtown has had its share of redevelopment experiments.

A Community Redevelopment Agency was created in the 1980s to spur development in Overtown and the Omni areas of Miami. The agency, funded in part by property taxes, has come under fire in recent months for what critics say is wasteful spending, with very little to show. In fact, McKnight and others launched an unsuccessful effort to recall Miami Commissioner Arthur Teele Jr., the CRA's board chairman.

"There will be no tears shed by the residents of this community if the CRA goes. It means and has meant nothing to them," McKnight said. "It could have been the panacea that brought them out of the water. Instead, it brought them parking lots, and we're still riding bicycles."

Teele could not be reached for comment.

In recent years, the area was also designated as an empowerment zone, qualifying for state and federal dollars to boost development. But the state has repeatedly refused to match the federal contributions to get projects started.

Urban revitalization projects are not new. Several states, including Florida, have created enterprise zones, where businesses receive tax credit for investing in poor neighborhoods. Michigan recently created a "renaissance zone" that offers sales-tax and other tax exemptions for the first few years. Taxes are then phased in.

The project stands out, says Rivera and Diaz de la Portilla, because of the 10-year span and because there is little government involvement.

Several states, including Florida, have created enterprise zones, where businesses receive tax credit for investing in poor neighborhoods.

No Input in Past

"A lot of people have imposed potential solutions on Overtown without incorporating or gathering input from the residents," Rivera said. "This takes government out of the picture."

Though the state would lose at least $6 million in sales tax revenue each year based on his proposal, he believes it would reap benefits in the long term because taxpayers would no longer have to support programs to prop up the poor.

The proposal also has the blessing of Democratic Rep. Dorothy Bendross-Mindingall, whose district includes Overtown.

"I applaud this gentleman for looking across party lines and across neighborhoods. I don't know why he's doing it, I'm just glad he's doing it," she said.

Still, several members of the Miami-Dade delegation are not sold on the idea.

Gus Barreiro, a Republican legislator whose district includes Little Havana, another poor neighborhood, says he would be very hesitant to support the proposal for a number of reasons.

Excluded

He says neighborhoods like Little Havana will wonder why they weren't included.

But even more troubling, Barreiro said, is that businesses may flock to the area en masse just to avoid paying sales taxes.

"If we're not careful, Overtown could become the flea market of Dade County. These residents could get pushed out. I don't see how this plan balances growth with the needs of the homeowners," he said.

Sen. Frederica Wilson, D-Miami, says she, too, is worried that the residents will somehow get left behind. Plus, the requirement that businesses hire at least 20 percent of their workforce from the neighborhood is a "pittance," she says.

"Anytime you try to expand or give special amenities to business as tax breaks, my antennas go up," Wilson said.

Urban renewal projects are often disguised as a way to help minorities but often lead to gentrification.

"Are we trying to build a black community or are we trying to build up Miami?" Wilson asked. "It seems to me that is about the expansion of downtown, and this is the only way they can expand without going into the bay."

III. Transportation Infrastructure

Editor's Introduction

For the majority of Americans, traffic jams and congested city streets have become a way of life. As the population has grown, so has the number of automobiles on the road—at a far greater rate than new roads and lanes are being added to the existing infrastructure. For drivers this has meant increasing frustration over delays and inconsistent commuting times, not to mention the phenomenon of "road rage," a term that surfaced in the 1990s to describe the aggressive and occasionally violent behavior triggered, presumably, by the agonies of sitting in traffic that creeps along for mile after mile. The articles in this section introduce some of the transportation problems the country faces and some of the solutions available to urban planners.

In the first article of this section, "Gridlock Nation," Joan Lowy offers this dire bit of advice: "The next time you are stuck in a traffic jam, take a good look around and consider yourself lucky; it's only going to get worse." Lowy reports on recent concerns that existing transportation infrastructure will be insufficient to handle the pressures of the growing population in the decades ahead. In the ongoing debate among politicians and planners over how best to handle the problem, some argue that simply building more highways only increases congestion, a theory known as "induced demand." Responding to such arguments, Congress in recent years has given local communities more flexibility over how they spend federal transportation funding, allowing for investment in public transit and other alternatives. On the other side of the debate are those who say that failing to significantly expand the nation's highway system ignores the realities of growth. In addition, advocates say that construction projects on constricted thoroughfares can reduce air pollution and save millions of gallons of wasted fuel by cutting back on the amount of time automobiles spend idling in traffic. (See Appendix C on page 171 for a map showing the percentage change in traffic congestion in major urban areas between 1982 and 1997.)

Another alternative is proposed in the following article, "Fighting Traffic Congestion with Information Technology," by Martin Wachs, a professor of city and regional planning and the Roy W. Carlson Distinguished Professor of Civil and Environmental Engineering at the University of California at Berkeley, as well as the director of the university's Institute of Transportation Studies. Wachs provides an in-depth analysis of America's traffic woes, beginning with the fact that while solutions to congestion exist, such as "congestion pricing," they remain politically unviable. Congestion is, after all, a mixed blessing; it is frustrating, but it is associated with economic vitality and prosperity, not decline. After looking at the history of transportation and congestion, Wachs finds it unlikely that government policy will advocate the continued expansion of roadway networks, but he also points to the limits of smart growth, which he says "does reduce overall automobile travel, but it does so by creating congestion rather than relieving it." A solution may be found in applications of information technology, such as detectors and cameras to monitor and manage traffic flows, and the use of global positioning satellite (GPS) systems to keep track of vehicle locations.

The recent emergence of new light-rail transit systems in such unlikely sprawl centers as Dallas, Houston, and Phoenix is the subject of "All Aboard" by Jane Holtz Kay, author of the book *Asphalt Nation* and a noted critic of America's automobile culture. Kay sees these developments as the result of an increased distaste for sprawl, even in southwestern cities that have traditionally resisted transit development. She notes that large segments of the public are still reluctant to designate funding for new transit projects: in Phoenix voters went several rounds before approving a four-cent sales tax to fund the area's Valley Connections light rail. In Dallas, however, support is strong. In 1996 Dallas Area Rapid Transit (DART) added to its network a 20-mile light-rail transit system, which has since achieved a daily ridership of over 38,000, and in August 2000 more than 77 percent of the voters approved a plan for about $3 billion in long-term funding for DART's light-rail projects.

In addition to managing the constant demand for new roads and added highway lanes, cities are continually engaged in the ongoing process of freeway redevelopment. One of the most notorious freeway construction projects currently in the works is Boston's Artery Project, also known as the Big Dig. As Robert Campbell, Pulitzer Prize-winning architecture critic for the *Boston Globe*, explains in the final article of this section, the Big Dig is a multi-billion-dollar project, now in its final stages, to build an underground tunnel for Boston's Central Artery, a worn-down and congested elevated expressway. While critics have complained of huge cost overruns—after initial estimates of $2.6 billion in 1983, the price has grown to about $15 billion today—others say it will be worth the investment, improving traffic flow, boosting downtown real estate, and healing the blighted region with parks and other developments. (The tables in Appendix D, starting on page 172, provide U.S. Census Bureau figures indicating what total percentage of the working population in the U.S. uses which form of transportation to get to work, such as driving alone, carpooling, and taking public transit. Travel times to work are listed as well. The same information is provided for the counties of two selected cities mentioned in articles in this chapter—Dallas, Texas, and Boston, Massachusetts.)

Gridlock Nation[1]

By Joan Lowy
The Record, July 15, 2001

The next time you are stuck in a traffic jam, take a good look around and consider yourself lucky; it's only going to get worse.

For decades, increases in traffic congestion have outpaced attempts to expand the nation's transportation infrastructure on the ground and in the air. Despite two major legislative efforts by Congress during the 1990s to beef up that infrastructure, some transportation and urban policy experts predict the United States is headed toward a "congestion crisis" that could have serious consequences for the economy.

"We are approaching an impending capacity crisis where demand threatens to overwhelm our existing transportation systems," said William Millar, president of the American Public Transportation Association.

The 2000 census figures released this year, which show the U.S. population grew by 32 million people in the last decade and will gain 120 million people by 2050, for a total population exceeding 400 million, were a "wake-up call" for transportation planners, says Dean Carlson, secretary of the Kansas Department of Transportation and president of the American Association of State Highway and Transportation Officials.

Driving, as measured by the amount of vehicle miles per person, has been going up even faster than the population almost every year. So has the number of cars on the highways. Between 1980 and 1997, the United States added 1.2 cars or trucks for every additional person. At that rate, there will be 48 million to 62 million more vehicles on the road by 2020, estimated Anthony Downs, a senior fellow at the Brookings Institution think tank.

Downs is among a growing number of urban policy and transportation experts who believe that congestion is going to continue to worsen even if the nation builds more roads and adds more public transit.

"This is a problem without a solution, at least no solution the American public will accept," Downs recently testified before the House Transportation and Infrastructure Committee. "My advice is that everyone should get used to being stuck in traffic some of the time.

"You should get a climate-controlled car with a stereo radio and tape deck and CD player, a hands-free telephone, a fax machine, and even a microwave oven, and commute each day with someone you really like."

---

1. © Scripps Howard News Service

The situation has alarmed business and industry leaders, who fear that without even greater federal expenditures on new roads and airports, some areas of the country may reach a point where they are unable to effectively move goods and people.

Last month, the U.S. Chamber of Commerce announced the formation of a new lobbying coalition of transportation industries and users, Americans for Transportation Mobility, whose aim is to pry more money out of Congress for highway and airport projects when lawmakers begin work next year on the next five-year transportation construction bill.

"If you go around the country, you will see construction projects that have been started . . . but we're so far behind and that's why we have road rage and air rage and all kinds of other rages," Rep. Don Young, R-Alaska, House transportation committee chairman, said at a kick-off luncheon for the new coalition. "It's a social problem. It's also an environmental problem. Over 6.6 billion gallons of gasoline [were] spent last year sitting still."

But many transportation experts, urban planners, and environmentalists contend that nothing short of a fundamental change in where and how we live will turn the problem around.

That means moving away from the car-oriented culture that has marked America since World War II. It means building and redesigning "smart growth" communities that are high-density and mix housing with retail and office development so that walking, biking and taking public transit are realistic alternatives to congested highways. It means more telecommuting and flexible work hours. It means rethinking public transit in metropolitan areas so that trains and buses go more places people want to go, rather than just to and from city centers.

And it also may mean "congestion pricing," a concept that is already being tried in New York City, San Diego, and other metropolitan areas.

Congestion pricing is aimed at weeding some drivers off the road by applying higher tolls or surcharges for using highways, bridges and tunnels at peak hours.

One thing many experts believe should not happen is massive new highway construction, which they say worsens congestion. The theory, called "induced demand," is that new highways built to accommodate suburban sprawl or to reduce congestion create only temporary relief as drivers quickly fill up the open roads until traffic is as crowded as before.

"If you build it, they will come," says Jeff Anderson, director of the development, community and environment division at the Environmental Protection Agency. "Most people nationally are seeing that road-building by itself has not been an effective solution."

Responding to smart-growth advocates, Congress gave local communities in the 1992 and 1998 funding bills greater flexibility over how they spend federal transportation dollars so that they can use the money for public transit and other alternatives to driving rather than simply on highway construction.

"I don't think we can build roads forever in order to increase our transportation capacity so that our society works," says Bill Fulton, president of Solimar Research Group, a metropolitan growth policy analysis firm in Ventura, Calif. "The way to think about it is that we are not alleviating congestion; we are increasing capacity.

"We can't build another whole interstate system, we can't plow freeways through every neighborhood in this country, we have to do different things to increase our capacity to move goods, information, and people and provide access. That's what all these other alternatives are all about."

But failing to increase the nation's highway system in a substantial way ignores the realities of growth, says U.S. Chamber of Commerce President Tom Donohue.

"The arguments that say, 'If we don't build it, they won't come,' just don't carry any water," Donohue says. "They are coming. They

---

It's unrealistic to expect people to completely give up their cars or not to build any new roads at all.

---

are here. And we have got to build an infrastructure or we're going to be in a California situation." It's unrealistic to expect people to completely give up their cars or not to build any new roads at all, Fulton agreed. Nevertheless, Americans need to change fundamental expectations, he said.

"Traffic engineers have set up an expectation for us that even if we live in the middle of an immensely large and densely populated metropolitan area that we should be able to get on the freeway almost immediately and go 60 mph to almost anywhere we want," Fulton said. "I think that's an unrealistic expectation for an urban society."

Americans for Transportation Mobility plans to spend millions of dollars on a television ad campaign aimed at convincing voters of the need for more transportation construction. The campaign will emphasize the environmental benefits of road construction, Donohue said.

A study by the industry-funded American Highway Users Alliance concluded that construction improvements to 170 major traffic bottlenecks could sharply reduce air pollution and save millions of gallons of fuel.

"That sounds a lot better to me than the Kyoto treaty," said Dono-hue, referring to the international accord aimed at reducing greenhouse gas emissions. "We can't allow the antigrowth people to use layer and layer and layer of environmental arguments to prevent us from building the infrastructure that will in fact reduce pollution."

Environmentalists, however, contend that new road construction, as opposed to maintaining and improving existing roads, increases, not lessens, pollution.

"Alleviating bottlenecks can sometimes have a short-term benefit for cutting pollution and fuel use," said Michael Replogle, an urban-sprawl expert at Environmental Defense, "but that is rapidly offset by the induced traffic that fills up the wider roads. The traffic count monitors corroborate that."

Fighting Traffic Congestion with Information Technology[2]

By Martin Wachs
Issues in Science and Technology, Fall 2002

Traffic congestion is a vexing problem felt by residents of most urban areas. Despite centuries of effort and billions of dollars' worth of public spending to alleviate congestion, the problem appears to be getting worse. Between 1980 and 1999, vehicle-miles of travel on U.S. roadways grew by 76 percent, while lane miles increased by only 3 percent. Average daily vehicular volumes on urban interstates rose by 43 percent between 1985 and 1999, from 10.331 million to 14.757 million. In a study of 68 urban areas published in 2001, the Texas Transportation Institute reported that the percentage of daily travel taking place during congested periods increased from 32 percent in 1982 to 45 percent in 1999; typical motorists faced seven hours per day of congested roadways in 1999 compared with five hours in 1982. According to the Federal Highway Administration, road delays (defined as travel time in excess of that at free flow conditions) increased by 8.5 percent between 1993 and 1997. Congestion also pollutes the air and wastes precious fuel.

Despite the exasperation that traffic congestion causes, most people know surprisingly little about it or what can be done about it, and much of what is stated in the media is oversimplification. We live in a society in which, for political and social reasons, we consistently label congestion a major problem to be solved but find it unacceptable to adopt the most effective solutions. Indeed, the political debate over the issue indicates that we actually prefer the problem to the solutions. If our current path continues, in the coming years we will implement innovations to mitigate worsening traffic and expand the transportation system to accommodate growth in travel to some extent, but we will likely shy away from measures that will literally cure the problem.

There is one factor, however, with the potential to change the course that we are on: information technology. There are a wide variety of applications of information technology that are just beginning to be implemented that could be far more significant in our struggle to defeat traffic congestion than the building of new

2. Reprinted with permission from *Issues in Science and Technology*, Wachs, "Fighting Traffic Congestion with Information Technology," Fall 2002, pp. 43–50, Copyright 2002 by the University of Texas at Dallas, Richardson, TX.

highways and transit routes or more government regulation. In fact, we now have the technical means to finally "solve" the congestion problem.

Mixed Blessing

Although we always label congestion a problem to be solved, it is surely not all bad. In the United States, worsening traffic congestion is most often associated with prosperity rather than poverty and with growth in population and business rather than decline. Congested city centers are usually the most exciting and high-rent of all urban environments, home to dynamic industries, tourist attractions, and cultural activities. Traffic congestion becomes less pronounced during recessions, and stagnant rust belt cities would willingly trade high unemployment rates and vacant industrial tracts for some troublesome traffic congestion. When and where it reaches very high levels, traffic congestion can become self-correcting; for example, when businesses choose to leave an area because it is too crowded and plagued by delays.

In the United States, worsening traffic congestion is most often associated with prosperity rather than poverty.

Politicians, not surprisingly, want to have their cake and eat it too. They want the growth and economic vitality that bring congestion, yet they also want to control or reduce that congestion. They worry that congestion will kill the goose that laid the golden egg by slowing growth and driving investment elsewhere, but refuse to implement effective strategies to relieve congestion because stringent solutions might, like congestion itself, redirect growth to other areas. Although technical experts could actually solve the problem of congestion, their solutions are politically unacceptable because they threaten economic growth along with congestion. In theory, automobiles could be banned from sectors of city centers; bridge tolls could be raised to such high levels that they would reduce traffic backups; and taxes on gasoline could be made so high that people would increasingly use mass transit and cycling. But such strategies could not be adopted in the United States and would stifle the economic growth and cultural activity that are considered the greatest successes of our society. Would we really vote for emptier streets if they meant fewer bargains at stores, closed movie houses, and higher rates of unemployment?

The notion that growing traffic has to be accommodated rather than stifled has been the motivation for innovations by private entrepreneurs and public officials over many centuries. The more successful of these have indeed reduced or eliminated congestion in some ways and for some time, but eventually cities have grown and readjusted to create a new equilibrium that includes new and perhaps different patterns of congestion. Then these are again identified as serious problems in need of repair, and new solutions are proposed. That process continues today, and although congestion has never actually been permanently alleviated by any of these innovations, they have surely improved the quality of urban life by supporting the expansion of diverse activity centers.

Policymakers usually base their recommendations on statements about congestion that consistently and dramatically oversimplify reality. In some cases, the beliefs that motivate policymaking may actually be dead wrong. Do we really know the extent to which citizens worry about traffic congestion or see it as a serious public policy problem? The evidence is confusing at best. Residents of the San Francisco Bay area recently rated urban traffic congestion as the single most important problem affecting their quality of life, even more important than public education or crime. This is consistent with research findings indicating that driving in heavy traffic is stressful, as measured by elevated blood pressure, eye pupil dilation, and the occurrence of incidents of road rage. On the other hand, there is also recent research showing that many people find driving to be a relaxing interlude between their many other stressful activities. Survey research recently has shown that a substantial proportion of drivers would actually prefer to spend more time traveling each day than they presently do. Presumably, a diversity of personality types and differences in our attitudes based on the time of day at which we travel and the purposes of our trips mean that it is difficult to generalize.

A substantial proportion of drivers would actually prefer to spend more time traveling each day than they presently do.

Press releases from transportation agencies and political leaders frequently speak of tens of millions of dollars in annual "costs" associated with congestion in metropolitan areas. Where do such numbers come from, and what do they mean? These estimates come quite simply from multiplying aggregate hours of delay by some dollar figure such as a "typical" hourly wage rate: A million hours of delay per year times $10 per hour yields a cost of congestion of $10 million, a dramatic figure quickly reported by the news media. But it is not at all clear that this number has any meaning. Some drivers, like those behind the wheels of commercial vehicles, are indeed paid wages for time they spend on the road, but most are not. And if we could produce a miracle that would enable us tomorrow to spend much less time in congested traffic than we did today, would we actually convert the saved time into labor that would produce added income? For most of us the answer would be no, so the wage rate may be a meaningless way to value congestion. If we used the saved time to mow the lawn or go for a jog, the time saving would certainly have value, but is that value appropriately expressed by a wage rate?

It is similarly not clear that if one citizen loses 10 minutes a day whereas another loses 100 minutes to congestion, that the second person's loss is worth 10 times that of the first person. We may not be willing to pay anything to save 10 minutes per day but willingly pay to save 100 minutes, so the value of time may be quite nonlinear, complicating the situation greatly.

As we learn more about travel behavior, we have begun to understand that travelers are more interested in the predictability of the time that a trip takes than they are in the average length of trip time. In other words, people are not likely to complain as much if a trip takes them on average 45 minutes instead of 30 minutes, but they are likely to be quite concerned if it takes 15 minutes one day and 45 minutes the next. To avoid being late to work or to an important appointment, we must plan a trip to allow for the longest travel time that can reasonably be expected rather than for an average travel time. Aggregate hours of delay may very poorly measure what is most important to people about traffic congestion, and attaching dollar values may obfuscate rather than clarify the issue. Census data show us that the median journey from home to work in the United States is increasing by only a few minutes per decade, even though cities are spreading out considerably. People in the suburbs travel longer distances between home and work than do those in the inner city, but generally they make those trips at higher speeds, so travel times are growing very slowly. In the face of this evidence that typical travel time is hardly growing, it is probably our concern with the variance or reliability of travel time that explains our growing concern about traffic congestion. Interestingly, although variance is more important than median travel time, we collect data on the median and report nothing to the public about the variation.

Policymakers also have a poor understanding of the mechanics of traffic congestion, which is highly localized in time and space. Well over 90 percent of our roads are uncongested for well over 90 percent of the time. Some congestion—indeed, up to a third of all traffic delay—is caused by incidents that are difficult to predict, such as accidents, spilled loads, or construction equipment. Recurrent congestion, caused by demand outstripping capacity, occurs mostly at busy activity centers and important bottlenecks such as bridges, tunnels, and critical intersections. When overall congestion becomes worse, however, it generally does not become more intense at locations that are already heavily congested; rather, it spreads over longer periods each day and to additional locations. Drivers can often avoid congestion by choosing alternate routes or times at which to travel, but as many people leave earlier or later for work or choose an uncongested boulevard in preference to a crowded expressway, they gradually cause congestion to build at those times and on those alternative routes.

Traffic congestion is also nonlinear, meaning that when volume doubles or triples on a lightly traveled street the effect on travel times is minimal, whereas adding just a few cars and trucks to a crowded roadway causes large increases in delay. This explains why traffic seems to be much worse on the day that school reopens in the fall and to be surprisingly light in New York or Boston on Jewish holidays. Adding or removing only a small fraction of all travelers can make an enormous differences in traffic flow, which makes traffic eminently subject to management strategies. Although congestion is nonlinear, people think in linear ways; congestion on a major bridge leads to calls for another bridge, even though small adjustments could quite dramatically reduce delay.

A Long History

Congestion is not a new phenomenon, and every civilization has developed innovative solutions to control or accommodate it. In ancient Rome, the Caesars noted that the passage of goods carts on narrow city streets so congested them that they became impassable and unsafe for pedestrians. A government edict required goods vehicles to make deliveries at night, but this policy was soon overturned because citizens complained that their sleep was interrupted by the sounds of vehicles traversing the pavement and of animals straining under their loads. Charles II of England issued a famous edict in 1660 to ban standing carriages, wagons, and horses from the streets of Westminster and London because they were excessive and were creating a public nuisance. He ordered that they be required to wait for their passengers off the main thoroughfares to enable the traffic to flow more freely on the boulevards.

Industrialization brought urbanization, and 19th-century cities were incredibly crowded places. Most people walked to work or lived above or behind their businesses, and rudimentary horse-drawn public transit was too expensive for most citizens. Population densities in industrial cities were many times what they are today, and urban congestion was then widely understood to mean the crowding of people in limited space. By the late 19th century, the high density of dwelling units, high occupancy of residential quarters, proximity of living areas to working areas, environmental hazards of factories, and transportation systems based on animal power were together defined as congestion. The innovation that addressed this problem was improved public transportation, first on the surface and powered by horses; later elevated or underground and powered by cables, steam, and eventually electricity. Affordable and reliable public transportation meant that people could live farther from where they worked and travel much more. At first, only the rich could move away from the center, but gradually fares fell in relation to incomes, and more and more people could commute to work. At the first national Conference on Planning and the Problems of Congestion nearly 100 years ago, speakers urged lower densities and the deliberate suburbanization of the population. In New York, zoning was introduced in part to lower the land use intensity so as to ease overcrowding. The flat subway fare (meaning that the fare was the same for a 20-mile journey as for a 1-mile trip) was adopted to encourage lower-income people to move out of the city center and new immigrants to locate in outlying neighborhoods, which were considered safer and more healthful than the crowded downtown areas.

As more people moved out of the centers of large cities and relied on public transportation, the perception of congestion changed from crowded neighborhoods to crowded streetcars on tracks so filled with trolley cars that movement was extremely slow. Innovations that helped ease this new form of crowding included the construction of the first urban elevated routes and, just before 1900, the development of underground transit routes, along with the development of signaling systems to control complex flows in the transit networks. Grade separation of vehicles with passengers from pedestrians and horse-drawn goods vehicles provided the capacity for more movement within cities, permitting both growth and decentralization.

Rapid declines over just a few decades in the cost of auto ownership in relationship to worker wages meant that many more people became mobile. Automobiles provided an order-of-magnitude increase in movement capacity and meant that cities could continue to grow and spread. The most rapid growth rates in automobile ownership and driver's license holding occurred between 1910 and the Great Depression, and city streets became very crowded with motor vehicles during that time. Innovations devised during this period by engineers, politicians, and bureaucrats included the widening of roads and the rationalization of street networks by, for example, straightening streets and making them more continuous with one another. Busy intersections gradually came to be managed by signs and mechanical signals that were eventually replaced by electric signals that later were coordinated with one another into systems that accommodated higher traffic volumes. Proposals for access-controlled and grade-separated roadways also originated in this period, but years of depression and war slowed their adoption as automobile ownership and use continued to grow. After World War II, prosperity returned and growth picked up in employment, the economy, and travel. In response to dramatic increases in congestion, the federal government in the 1950s planned, and over 40 years built, a national system of "interstate and defense highways," encouraging state governments to build more than 40,000 miles of freeways by providing them with more than 90 percent of the money. Roadway capacity for a short while grew faster than motor vehicle travel, so this growth in new capacity seemed to solve the problem of congestion, but population and economic activity also expanded; land use became more dispersed; and, as the statistics in the opening paragraph indicate, over time goods movement and passenger travel have grown to utilize and surpass the capacity of the road network.

During the past 20 years, the costs of new highway capacity have become political liabilities that exceed its benefits. Community disruption, land taking, decentralization of population, production of air pollution, and dependence of the automobile and highway system on petroleum energy sources all limit the likelihood that government policy will emphasize continued expansion of roadway networks. It is now common to say that we cannot build our way out of congestion, because new roads induce new traffic. Whereas decentralization of the city was to another generation the solution for congestion, many today urge that we slow the pace of suburbanization by promoting "smart growth" that includes dense commercial and residential nodes of development at transit stations. Whereas road construction was to another generation the solution to traffic congestion, today it is just as often seen to be the cause of the problem.

The Limitations of Smart Growth

Environmentalists and urban planners have adopted smart growth as the ultimate solution to congestion. They urge that we cluster development near transit stations, increase urban densities, and mix land use, including putting stores and housing together, so that people can live without relying so much on their cars. By redirecting growth back into the city center, they believe that more people will be able to walk and use public transit and that automobile use will decline. This approach appeals to intellectuals, who are often fond of the kinds of environments found in downtown New York, Boston, and San Francisco, and their proposals are exciting for many reasons. Those reasons, however, do not include potential reductions in congestion. In fact, this strategy seems to confuse the solution with the problem. Should we emulate Hong Kong, Tokyo, or Manhattan as the strategy for alleviating congestion?

Environmentalists and urban planners have adopted smart growth as the ultimate solution to congestion.

It is true that low-density environments create more vehicle miles of driving per capita or per household than high-density environments. Without doubt, people are more likely to walk and use public transit in dense, mixed-use urban neighborhoods, but they are likely to do so in part because those neighborhoods are seriously congested. Can congestion be seen as the cure for congestion? Yes, but only in part. A strategy that creates more dense, mixed-use, transit-oriented communities and fewer low-density suburban neighborhoods can reduce vehicular travel in the aggregate, but at the expense of greater congestion in our city cores. A suburban neighborhood that contains five dwelling units per acre might produce 10 person-trips per day per household, which by simple arithmetic means 50 trips per acre per day, few or none of which would be made by walking or public transit. An urban neighborhood with 20 dwelling units per acre might, by contrast, produce only seven person-trips per household, but the same arithmetic shows that this neighborhood would produce 140 trips per acre per day. If 10 or 20 percent of these trips were made by walking or public transportation, the urban neighborhood would still produce more automobile traffic per acre than the suburban neighborhood. In other words, smart growth does reduce overall automobile travel, but it does so by creating congestion rather than relieving it. This is not necessarily bad, but it implies that many planners and environmentalists are disingenuous when they urge us to fight congestion through smart growth. Like the politicians, they really want more congested environments but presumably want that congestion to be somehow managed and accommodated. If it is not accommodated, people will start to move to the suburbs specifically to avoid congestion, and that will create more reliance on automobiles.

Applying Information Technology

What we choose to do about worsening congestion in the next few decades will be a product of the long and complex history of multiple innovations outlined above and also of the types of innovations and technology that characterize the current era. If history teaches us any lessons, it is that the effectiveness of available technical innovations will be tempered and directed by political priorities and interpretations of what is possible and desirable. Today there is little political will to dramatically expand existing highway networks and little support for extreme measures, such as vehicle restrictions that could control congestion but stifle economic growth. A large proportion of available transportation resources will be needed to maintain, replace, and repair our existing aging highway and transit networks, leaving little money to spend on new roads or expanded transit systems.

At the same time, the major force influencing the world economy in recent years has been information technology (IT). Rapid and extensive integration of IT with the transportation network is already underway and is the key to the management of congestion growth. Thus far, however, the accomplishments are quite modest in comparison with the possibilities.

Travelers today can receive directions to their destinations in their vehicles on handheld computers or by using devices incorporated into their dashboards. Most currently available information is similar to a traditional road atlas in that route information is not yet modified by data on current traffic conditions. For 30 years, traffic and transportation authorities have been gradually incorporating instruments into roadways and vehicles to provide increasingly useful information for managing traffic flows. "Loop detectors" buried under arterial streets and freeways report on traffic density, and the data they collect are being used to estimate speeds and travel times with increasing accuracy. In some cities, these data are being used to optimize the timing of traffic signals in order to maximize flows on segments of street networks. Cameras located on bridges and over busy intersections complement the data collected from the detectors to feed visual images of incidents to traffic control centers from which tow trucks and emergency vehicles can be dispatched when needed.

Thus far, most applications of this technology have enabled us to improve the management of parts of the transportation system in real time on the basis of information on current flows. Because traffic patterns repeat themselves day after day, techniques are emerging that will soon enable us to merge historical data with information taken from the monitoring of current flows to predict traffic patterns with increasing accuracy over the coming minutes and hours. This information will in the near future be made available to potential travelers over the Internet and through cell phones, car radios, or dashboard display screens to those already on the road.

> *The application of IT will allow us to better manage traffic flows to save travelers time and money.*

The extent to which the application of IT will allow us to better manage traffic flows to save travelers time and money is in the longer term more likely to be limited by political and social considerations than it is by the technology itself. For example, it is technologically feasible to track vehicle locations and to provide drivers with specific information on the current and projected traffic levels and travel times on several alternate routes. However, concerns about intrusion into personal privacy could limit the use of this innovation.

Because they present fewer challenges to privacy and produce greater gains in efficiency, these technologies will more quickly be applied to trucks and public transit vehicles. Operators of truck fleets and transit operators already use Automatic Vehicle Location (AVL) technology that employs Global Positioning Satellite Systems (GPSS) to keep track of the location of vehicles on city streets. Trucks can be programmed while in service for additional pickups and deliveries based on their current locations, and this type of information is increasingly used to tell bus drivers to bypass certain stops in order to fill gaps in service. Through display terminals at bus stops or through cell phone access, this type of information is also beginning to be used to provide bus users with information on the expected arrival time of the vehicle they hope to board. Such innovations will help us manage traffic congestion, and many believe that applications of "intelligent transportation systems" can accommodate up to half of the growth in congestion that will occur over the coming decades. That's impressive, but is it enough?

Congestion Pricing

In the past, the vast majority of the costs of building and operating transportation systems have been paid through a system of user fees. Tolls are the most direct user fees, with fuel taxes really functioning as surrogate tolls, because they collect money roughly in proportion to how much we drive. When fuel taxes were adopted more than 80 years ago, they were seen as inferior to tolls because they didn't levy charges at the location and time of travel. But fuel taxes had lower costs of administration; just a few percent of the fuel tax is spent to cover the costs of collecting the money, whereas the cost to operate tollbooths often amounted to a quarter of the tolls collected.

> *It is theoretically possible to eliminate congestion through pricing.*

Americans are by and large not even aware that as much as one-third of the cost of gasoline at the pump is a charge (technically a fee rather than a tax) used to cover the costs of building, maintaining, and managing roads and transit systems. Over time, however, improved vehicle fuel economy and political reluctance to raise the price of gas have reduced the fiscal productivity of these fees. In the near future, hybrids, electric cars, and fuel cell–powered vehicles may make fuel taxes obsolete as a source of funds with which to finance the transportation system. This apparent problem could actually be the key to finally solving the problem of highway congestion.

Economists have long argued that the only way to completely solve the congestion problem is through congestion pricing. Economic theory says that the price of traveling should be higher at the places and times of day when demand for (and benefit from) using them is greatest. If it were to cost, for example, three times as much to pay a bridge toll at the period of highest congestion as it does in the middle of the night, some travelers would surely be more likely to use public transit, form carpools, use less crowded alternate routes, or reschedule less essential trips at off-peak hours. It is theoretically possible to eliminate congestion through pricing, because in principle the price can ultimately be raised to a level that is high enough to clear the traffic jam. There are now a dozen or more travel corridors throughout the world where variable pricing for travel is in use, including a small handful in the United States. Congestion pricing has been successfully used in Singapore for more than 25 years, and London is planning to implement such a system early in 2003.

Although transportation experts have written about congestion pricing for decades, one of the major obstacles to its implementation has long been the technical difficulty of collecting tolls: Building toll plazas and varying the charges with time of day and class of vehicle are complex, expensive, and politically problematic tasks. But the recent advances in IT now make congestion pricing much more technically feasible. Small inexpensive transponders, already in use in millions of vehicles to pay tolls, enable each motorist to be charged a different fee to use each segment of road at a particular time of day. The charges can appear on monthly credit card bills. I can envision a future in which the familiar "gasoline tax" is eliminated, especially because gasoline itself may have a limited future as a source of power in transportation. Instead, motorists would be charged more directly for the use of roadways through simple applications of IT.

We now have the technical capacity to integrate into one system the mechanisms for financing our highway system and controlling congestion. Charging more than we now do for the use of the busiest roads at the busiest times of day, and quite a bit less than we now do at other times, would be the fairest and most efficient way to raise the funds needed for operating and expanding the capacity of the transportation system. At the same time, we would use the charges to meter the use of the system to control congestion. Some argue that the accounting system needed for congestion pricing will be an invasion of privacy, but it is possible to prevent this by using numbered accounts. Others argue that congestion pricing discriminates against the poor. Yet the current system of transportation finance is not at all neutral with respect to income, and a system of direct charges for actual benefits gained from using the system is inherently fairer than a complex system of cross subsidies. For many trips, the proposed approach would provide for a lowering of trip costs in comparison with the current means of pricing travel. And it would surely be possible to offer lifeline rates to the poor.

Personal mobility and the transportation system will be deeply affected by IT during the coming decades. Many applications of IT to traffic congestion relief will be the product of innovations by private firms. Within just a few years, for example, and without government intervention, we will be reserving our parking spaces electronically as we approach airports and shopping centers, rather than cruising for an available vacant space.

Using history as a guide, it would seem that we have the technical means at hand with which to finally solve the congestion problem. Thus, the most significant determinants of the future use of IT for traffic control will be political rather than technical. Based on the history reviewed here, I believe that in approaching the future, the goal of policymakers should not be to eliminate traffic congestion but rather to try to strike a new balance between growth, congestion, and the political acceptability of the measures by which we can eliminate that congestion.

All Aboard³

By Jane Holtz Kay
Planning, October 2000

Could this be the post-automobile century?

Look around and you'll see light rail lines rolling off into the Phoenix desert, stretching along the Dallas plains, breaking ground in Salt Lake City, and drawing crowds in Denver.

Whether "rail lite" or a "new wave," this phenomenon marks the fourth generation of rail. The 19th century brought the first and primary generation, the gas-short 1970s defined the second, and the early 1980s and '90s expansion led by San Diego and Portland, the third. Now new lines are being built in the most car-oriented cities in the nation. Sprawl is the enemy, and local dollars the engine.

"It's growing," says Jeffrey Boothe, chair of the 55-city New Starts Working Group, a national coalition of transit agencies and organizations. According to the American Public Transit Association (APTA), applicants for federal "new starts" money have increased from 200 in 1992 to double that number now. With so many new applicants, the Federal Transit Administration has run short of funds to meet the demand, shifting from a federal-state funding ratio of 80–20 to 50–50.

The Converts

Phoenix and Houston, the last holdouts and largest cities lacking rail, have recently voted to move ahead. When Denver opened its 8.7-mile southwest corridor line in July, some 25,000 riders showed up on the very first day—and 35,000 on day two.

Nationwide, APTA cites a record 4.8 percent increase in ridership for the first quarter of the year, the highest peak in annual ridership since 1960. Locally initiated, community funded, and supported by federal funds, light rail during the first decade under the Intermodal Surface Transportation Efficiency Act (now TEA-21) saw an increase of 44.2 percent in miles of track. Transit trips are up a total of 15 percent in the last three years (compared with car trips at eight percent), says the Surface Transportation Policy Project (STPP) in Washington, D.C.

"It's gotten to the point where almost every city wants rail," says George Haikalis, president of the Institute for Rational Mobility in New York City.

Today's fourth and enlarged constituency of rail supporters ranges from the National Park Service, which wants to rim Grand Canyon, to middle-America Minneapolis, to office-park-studded Silicon Val-

---

ley. The several thousand people who attended the annual Rail-Volution conference in Dallas last year and Denver this month attest to the zeal for riding rail.

Watchwords

Only don't call them "streetcars" or "trolleys." It's "light rail," or LRT, say their builders. If there is one thing that characterizes the latest transit missionaries, it's their urge to separate themselves from the time-worn streetcars in the urban corridors their populations left behind.

Take Phoenix and Dallas. These newly converted light rail communities share the common characteristics of a paltry, car-glutted downtown combined with sprawl and the minimal density that makes the communities along the way barely worth a dot on any self-respecting transit map. Consult a diagram of Phoenix's forthcoming Valley Connections light rail or Dallas's up-and-running DART line and you are more likely to see jagged single lines—spiders joined to spiders—than the traditional hub-and-spoke or star systems of urban rail.

But these New West cities also share congestion, poor air quality, and burgeoning populations. Not to mention opponents of new roads—not only those that one Michigan road builder calls "the sandal-wearing quiche-eating environmental freakazoids" but also neighbors of more moderate persuasion who insist on pricey sound walls and plantings. "People have recognized that they don't have a lot of options," says Wulf Grote, project director of Phoenix's LRT.

Then there is ISTEA. While this 1991 law required planning bodies (COGs and MPOs), flexible funds, and enhancements that haven't quite lived up to expectations, its mandate that state departments of transportation perform a rigorous cost test for alternatives to every road project has slowed the pace of highway building, says STPP's executive director, Roy Kienitz.

If They Can Do It. . . .

What's happening in Phoenix and Dallas—poster children of sprawl—can happen elsewhere. Phoenix is now doing preliminary engineering for a new line, and Dallas is expanding its four-year-old DART line.

Phoenix, a weakling in public transportation, passed its first vote for light rail in March and is now in preliminary engineering for its first 20 miles and holding meetings with neighbors for 22 stations, to begin construction in 2003 and open three years later. Dallas, with its impressive 1996 installation of 20 miles of tracks (and 24 more in the pipeline), its stylish new cars, handsome stations, and transit-oriented projects, is the new mecca after Portland and San Diego.

In both Phoenix and Dallas, light rail benefited from a shift in demographics: the young seeking a livelier lifestyle and the old seeking an alternative to the automobile. Whether the light rail systems can stem sprawl, whether they can use their popularity to counter highway subsidies or not, the trend is there. So, of course, is the difficulty in getting the public to adopt, and pay for, public transit.

Phoenix: Ballot to Drawing Board

It wasn't exactly a boxing match, but voters in Phoenix's 450-square-mile transit service area went several rounds before saying "yes" to a .04 sales tax to fund the project. In 1997, reeling from a 122-vote defeat (out of 110,000 cast), Phoenix's transit supporters decided to focus on outreach, says Jyme Sue Olsen, principal planner with the Regional Public Transportation Authority (RPTA). Campaigners mailed out a six-page *Transit 2000* document filled with maps, graphs, and diagrams for new bus, rail, and public transit. Officials organized 10 public meetings in a two-year period and consulted with area businesses.

"What they were finding at all the meetings was that the employers were having a hard time getting workers," says Steve Beard, deputy project director of the RPTA, and "a lot of people were getting tired of sprawl." With Mayor Skip Rimska finally coming on board to help raise some $1.4 million and a meager $10,000 coming from the opposition, the "Vote Yes" crowd handily defeated the "DeRail the Tax" interests.

LIGHT RAIL PROJECT AREA

The first phase of Phoenix's newly approved light rail system will connect downtown with Sky Harbor Airport and the city of Tempe. Extensions could include surrounding suburbs.

The current bare-bones system, which lacked Sunday bus service until this summer, was essentially overhauled when Phoenix voted two-to-one to allocate 34 percent of the $1.6 billion, 20-year transit plan to light rail while enhancing the bus system. "Light rail 1, Nimby's 0," *Railway Age* wrote in describing the vote. "How often do you get a chance to contribute to something like that?" asks Deputy Mayor Jack Tevlin, looking proudly at the framed newspaper clip of the election night, when he serenaded the crowd with a rendition of "I've been working on the railroad."

The route as it has emerged for the first 20-mile segment stretches in a sort of capped "L" shape with the downtown core at the right angle and the line heading east toward Sky Harbor International Airport, then reaching the town of Tempe, home to Arizona State University. Tempe passed a .05 tax to share in the system. Designed to run at 10-to-15-minute intervals for some 18,000 passengers a day, the system is pinned to "activity" stops at population centers, replicating the bus route along Central Avenue, the city's highest employment concentration. Other extensions could include Mesa, Glendale, and Scottsdale.

Recent neighborhood meetings have brought Phoenix residents together to define these stops. "A first," says Marc Soronson, manager of environmental planning for the RPTA, describing the participatory process. "It's snowballing," says Neal Manske, public transit director, in describing Phoenix's "embryonic" transit area planning.

Some insiders are less sanguine. "A pretty anemic amount," former mayor Terry Goddard says of the estimated 18,000 riders expected to use the first leg of the Phoenix system. Goddard, who served from 1984 to 1990, is dismayed that the system will not hook directly into an existing terminal at Sky Harbor Airport to benefit from the three million flyers who travel through there each month.

> *"Rail isn't a panacea. You're talking about changing a culture."—* **Katherine Wisehart, Phoenix city planner**

Hurdles

Several factors could ground the Phoenix system's ambitions: the city's thinly settled neighborhoods, asphalt-wrapped malls, and less-than-vibrant downtown.

Michael Beyard, vice-president of the Urban Land Institute, agrees that light rail "can be a very powerful focus in terms of combating sprawl," but insists that infill is essential. "Just creating the transit is not going to create this sort of development," he says.

"It's going to take some work," says Katherine Wisehart, a planner for the city of Phoenix. "Rail isn't a panacea. You're talking about changing a culture."

Concerned about far flung development at the fringes, the Sierra Club secured a growth management initiative that will appear on next month's ballot—with 160,000 signatures in favor of growth boundaries and impact fees. "The idea of Phoenix is just to let things happen," says Sandy Bahr, conservation coordinator for the Sierra Club's Arizona chapter, calling the city "the epitome of leapfrog" development.

Magnets like the vast new Del Webb community of Anthem to the north, with its 35,000 acres of walled single-family houses plus a new supermall, seem the ultimate in unabated sprawl and unsupported transit. "An environmental nightmare," says Goddard.

Some Phoenix planners point to positive new approaches: an overlay zoning district, parking ordinances, and transit-oriented guidelines in the works as well as infill. "We're already seeing development interest along the light rail corridor," says Joy Mee, AICP, assistant director of planning. "It's going to take more than light rail to make it work," she says, "but it's a contributor."

Mark McLaren, landscape architect, planner, and RPTA facility consultant, notes the stronger market for multifamily housing and sees some shift in the city from the "snowbird" values of the 1950s to a condo/loft community with conservationist leanings. "It happened in Texas and it's going to happen here," he says.

Dallas and DART

A railroad crossroads city grown to maturity after World War II, Dallas has established its new corridor along the old one. Lacking the growth and land-use controls of Portland or San Diego, DART has shown what a modern city driven by the private sector can do for rail (or vice versa).

Good design helps. DART's first transit stops won a U.S. Department of Transportation honor award in June for the HOK Planning Group, which produced the prototype. Daily ridership is over 38,000, and construction has never ceased.

It may not be a moment too soon. The DART service area population is 1.8 million, but 2.8 million more residents are expected by 2025. Dallas is "one of the few cities that's dealing with sprawl," says Sheila Holbrook-White of Texas Civic Action. She also notes with approval that DART built its first leg in the southern part of the Dallas metro area, where a preponderance of lower-income people could benefit—and would provide the most riders.

Douglas Allen, DART's vice-president of planning and development, points to some telling numbers: $800 million in development within walking distance of the DART line; $860 million to build it. Another study by a University of North Texas economist cited a rise of 25 percent in property values around the stations between its 1996 opening and the beginning of this year.

DART's point man for transit-oriented development in the system's 700-square-mile service area is Jack Wierzenski, AICP, senior manager of planning studies and economic development. "It's always crowded," he notes happily as we visit neighborhood stations. The reasons? "Each [station] is unique," he says. "Each has a sense of place."

Wierzenski's list of loft conversions includes buildings ranging from the handsome 1924 Santa Fe Union station to vacant 1950s offices like the Southland Center tower, now the Adams Mark, a $200 million, 1,900-room hotel. Jack Guerra, chief planner for the city, applauds the preservation efforts, citing the Republic Tower, a one-million-square-foot 1950s building, soon to hold offices, retail, and perhaps residences. Guerra credits DART with making "downtown an agreeable place to live."

Soft Spots

Although this rider spent 20 minutes waiting for a midday train in the subsurface Mockingbird station three miles from downtown Dallas, this particular station is considered one of DART's most successful, with pricey apartments (penthouses at $5,000 a month), offices, shops, a restaurant, and an eight-screen Angelica theater to come.

Even farther out, at the Galatyn Park Station 12 miles from downtown in the town of Richardson, DART will wrap its transit plaza with a performing arts center, a Nortel office building, and other mixed uses. This station on the "Telecom Corridor," due for completion in 2002, will have no parking.

Other fringe area transit stations seem less likely to generate car-free facilities, because DART uses persuasion, not muscle, to influence developers. Also, the need for cooperation among 13 communities contributes to a system that ranges from meager to incomplete, depending on your perspective. "We're not a real restrictive environment here, and it really takes a success to attract developers," Wierzenski says.

That free-for-all development, plus a downtown defined more by underground tunnels than surface amenities, means that walking through portions of the well-groomed, four-station Downtown Transitway Mall is hardly your ultimate urban experience. "Moles underground," says Sue Bauman, vice-president of marketing and communications at DART. Extended along ever more tracks, the mall also suggests a lack of commitment to rail's need for density.

"The downtown is on a slow but steady track, but it's got a long way to go," says Christine Carlyle, AICP, the city's former assistant director of planning and development, who orchestrated revitalization. With five streets under construction and planners laboring to infuse stores and restaurants, the core could resuscitate, she says. "I don't think it's going to come back overnight," Carlyle says. "It's a slow process. Still, rail is a natural asset. It can bring things into the center."

Big D

As in Phoenix, Dallas's extensive land area complicates the transit story. "Talk of a growth ring is heard," says Carlyle, "but Dallas doubled its land mass in the sixties and seventies and that makes it difficult." Thus, transit-oriented planning is slow here, as in other Western cities, and highway building constant, symbolized by the attempt to construct the hotly contested $120 million Southwest Parkway by the Trinity River, vigorously opposed by neighborhood groups.

"This ain't Portland, I can tell you," Bauman concedes. "Texans are beginning to see sprawl is not good. But this is a very independent part of the country." Moreover, light rail officials and boosters hesitate to admit to any inherent conflict between roads and rail. "Choice" is their motto.

Optimism reigns. Housing has taken off, with 13,000 residences recorded within a mile radius of the central business district. "Dot.comers like lofts, like rail," says Wierzenski. "The notion in the West is that people have 'the New Choice,'" says Tad Savenour, a consultant who's gained an overview by integrating art work for rail lines in Seattle, Portland, and elsewhere.

Above all, he says, "light rail is not about getting people out of their cars but creating nodes of development. It has to be a value-added experience."

Long Haul

Will the western mentality of limitless space—and limitless choice—change as the population continues to boom? Although U.S. Rep. Tom DeLay (R-Texas) blocked long-term funding for Houston's light rail line, the city is going ahead and expects to use a sales tax to fund it.

It seems that Dallas has become the new model for such upstart lines. Starting in 1982, when concerns over the swelling suburbs motivated some Texans to try to rein in development, advocates toiled through five campaigns to get a vote for a one percent sales tax. "Texas in general and Dallas in particular is not the kind of city that you'd think would take rail to its heart," Bauman says, "but we couldn't build our way out with concrete."

With the passage of a one percent tax this summer, DART has indeed embraced rail. Seventy-seven percent of the voters okayed long-term funding: some $3.1 billion on 52 miles of extensions to Carrollton, fast-growing Las Colinas, and Pleasant Grove, plus light rail to Dallas-Fort Worth International Airport. "Faster or slower, we're going ahead," Bauman said before the August balloting. On August 12, the forward march of "the biggest bond ever passed in the state of Texas" confirmed her optimism. "It's all good news," she says.

The Big Dig

What's Up Under Boston?[4]

By Robert Campbell
Architectural Record, March 2002

It was back in the early 1970s that the idea first surfaced. What if we demolish the Central Artery, Boston's other Green Monster, the overhead expressway that slithers like a fat invading dragon through downtown Boston, cutting most of the city off from its waterfront? What if we put it in a tunnel underground? With the barrier of the expressway gone, we said, we'll be able to reconnect the city with its harbor in an era when waterfronts are becoming sites for recreation, rather than for shipping and industry. We'll improve traffic flow by correcting the Artery's notoriously dangerous crossing movements. We'll even be able to run a branch of the new tunnel out to the airport. We'll increase the value of the downtown real estate that now suffers from the blight of the Artery. And, anyway, we noted, the Artery is aging and rusting. From time to time a chunk of concrete falls out, landing like a meteorite from the sky.

It all sounded like Utopia. But some were skeptical. The city's wisest and wittiest voice, Congressman Barney Frank (then a state legislator), suggested gloomily: "Depress the Artery? It might be cheaper to raise the city." His words sound prescient today, as cost projections climb toward the $15 billion mark. Press and politicians are quick to speak of "cost overruns."

But, in fact, the Artery Project—the Big Dig, as Bostonians call it—is a bargain. In any East Asian or European city, it would attract little attention. Osaka and Hong Kong create new international airports on artificial islands in the ocean. Europe tunnels more than 20 miles beneath the English Channel. Only in the United States is it considered odd to make large public investments in the quality of urban life. Fifteen billion dollars works out to about one movie ticket per American per year over the life of the Big Dig. It's worth it. And as any architect can probably intuit, the "overruns" are fictions, because the initial estimates were fictions. It is not possible to know in advance what a project like this will cost. A feasibility study for the Big Dig would be like a feasibility study for a war. You can begin a war, but you can't know where it will end. Nobody foresaw—nobody could have foreseen—the problems that the Dig would encounter.

The Dig exists because of the political legerdemain of the late Thomas P. "Tip" O'Neill, Speaker of the House. But the concept is that of Fred Salvucci, the acknowledged godfather of the Big Dig, who was secretary of transportation under former governor and presidential candidate Michael Dukakis. (A local joke: "If you want to depress the Artery, just ask Dukakis to talk to it.") Salvucci came

> *Whatever else it is, the Dig is a thrilling adventure in engineering.*

up with the brainstorm that the Dig would be part of the Interstate Highway System. Thus it could be largely funded by the federal government. By means of who knows what horse trades, Tip O'Neill sold that concept to Congress, which overrode a veto by President Reagan. The initial estimates were, as much as anything, Tip's canny assessment of what his colleagues would swallow. As the cost predictably ballooned, the feds grew reluctant to keep paying, and the state today picks up most of the tab. The real downside of the Big Dig is the way it's draining funds from every other state public works project.

Whatever else it is, the Dig is a thrilling adventure in engineering. You have to think of the tunnel as a kind of serpent, swimming just beneath the surface of the city. Like sea serpents, it isn't straight. There are places where it humps up to within a few inches of the surface, and there are places where it sinks more than 100 feet down. It does this because it has to slither its way among an incredible welter of subway lines and underground utilities.

At one point a corner of South Station, Boston's massive old masonry train station, was temporarily propped up, so the tunnel could be shoehorned between the station above and a subway line below—while keeping all roads and rail lines fully operational and uninterrupted. Engineers couldn't make a cut here, because a cut would disrupt the rail lines. They had to bore the tunnel. But the soil, which like most of Boston is mostly fill, was found to be too soft to tunnel through. It would have collapsed into the hole, along with the railroad tracks. So the soil, acres of it, was temporarily frozen to a depth of many feet to permit the boring machines to function.

A whole series of works of architecture had to be designed simply to house the fans that would ventilate the tunnel. One of them received a National Honor Award from the AIA, and when it was found that conventional tunnel sections for the extension to the airport could not be floated beneath Boston's low bridges, the engineers created an entire 7-acre factory at the harbor's edge to manufacture steel box sections. Each weighed about the same as the Titanic, and each was floated across the water and (like the Titanic) sunk, using global positioning technology to place it with a margin of error of less than half an inch.

Through it all, the old overhead Central Artery, with all its ramps, continued to function. It will not be torn down until the eight-lane tunnel beneath it is complete. Traffic of all kinds—Amtrak, commuter trains, subways, cars, and trucks—continues to flow with remarkably little inconvenience. The coordinating engineers, Bechtel/Parsons Brinkerhoff, solved problem after problem—employing technology that had been developed and proved, more often than not, in Europe. They also, predictably, made some blunders. Water leaked into one of the tunnels. Less forgivably, part of a bridge had to be rebuilt when it was discovered that reinforcing rods were spaced too close together, so the concrete couldn't be forced in to bond with them.

What Happens When Freeways Come Down

By Charles Lockwood

Besides Boston, eight other U.S. cities have started or completed freeway redevelopment projects: Cincinnati; Duluth; Fort Worth; Hartford; Pittsburgh; Portland, Oregon; San Francisco; and Seattle. Several more projects should start shortly: Milwaukee, Portland (again), and San Francisco (again). Such projects mean considerable professional opportunities—and large fees—for architects and planners.

Three forces are driving this emerging trend. First, many downtown freeways are obsolete due to overcrowding, lack of maintenance, and decades of heavy use. Second, money is available from federal, state, and local sources. Third, although freeway redevelopment projects are never cheap, they can reap tremendous financial returns and quality-of-life improvements.

Freeway redevelopment projects take three forms.

Removal: The best-known example is San Francisco's late but not lamented elevated Embarcadero Freeway. San Francisco will also remove its equivalent of Boston's Central Artery near the Civic Center.

When outright removal is not a realistic option, cities can turn to two other strategies.

Relocation: Fort Worth is demolishing the downtown stretch of I-30. A replacement section I-30 was built a quarter of a mile to the south, well outside the downtown core.

Retrofit: Freeways that cannot be removed or relocated can still be retrofitted with new features such as Pittsburgh's 100-foot-wide, 4,000-foot-long Allegheny Riverfront Park, built beside and atop the Fort Duquesne Boulevard highway.

Of course, freeway redevelopments face potential roadblocks. They are incredibly expensive and prone to cost overruns and mismanagement. In addition, most government officials—and many architects—have not recognized this trend, or the opportunities it offers our cities, so design issues are not being debated, plans are not being made, and specific freeway redevelopment programs are not being formulated.

The obsolescence of scores of ill-located 1950s and 1960s downtown freeways is an extraordinary opportunity to repair the damage they have wreaked upon American cities. But, if freeways are rebuilt where they stand, this nascent trend could become the opportunity that got away.

The bridge in question—the Leonard P. Zakim Bunker Hill Bridge, a name that sounds like the political compromise it is— occurs where the Big Dig tunnel emerges from the ground and crosses the Charles River into Cambridge. Already, the bridge—not yet open to traffic—is a Boston landmark, dramatically lit in blue at night. It is a cable-stayed construction designed by Swiss engineer Christian Menn. It is unique among such bridges, so far as I know, in that it is asymmetrical. To solve the intricate traffic movements, two of its lanes are cantilevered out to one side. This oddity gives the bridge an engagingly lopsided informality. Not so engaging is the dumb detail at the top of each of the supporting concrete towers. They are arbitrarily sculpted into pyramids so as to rhyme, visually, with the Bunker Hill Monument nearby. It's a needless gesture that spoils the rigorous beauty of the engineering.

Visiting the Big Dig at its most spectacular, about two years ago, was very much like walking into the interior of a Piranesi engraving of a madhouse or prison. Many people commented on the resemblance. In the deeper places, where the tunnel was cut rather than bored, you'd stand at the bottom between two slurry walls and look upward as much as 120 feet, through tier upon tier of steel and concrete, with the light trickling down as if from another planet.

OK, flash forward to the present. The end of the Big Dig is at last in sight. Now everyone's attention is on another issue: What to do with the new long, winding corridor of space that currently lies in the shadow of the overhead Artery, but which will emerge when the Artery comes down? This is today the most hotly argued design question in Boston. In a small way, it's like what happened when the fortifications of Vienna and similar cities were torn down. What do you do with the new space?

Predictable forces are aligned. The Greenspace Alliance, a powerful group in Boston, believes that as much of the surface as possible should be green parkland, air and grass and shrubs and trees, a "lung for the city," in Olmsted's term. The Artery Business Committee, representing owners and other business interests in the area, would like to see cultural uses introduced to activate the space, perhaps with outdoor cafes and the like. Architects, in general, tend to think metaphorically of sewing the city back together over this gash, rather than memorializing it by means of an uninterrupted linear park. (However, nothing exceeding a few stories can be economically built, since the tunnel isn't structured to bear anything higher.) The Horticultural Society would like to build a glazed winter garden, but it may not have the money to do so. The North End neighborhood at one end and the Chinese community at the other have their own agendas. The state legislature, in a virtually secret move, determined that the land will be called "The Rose Kennedy Greenway," honoring the matriarch of the Kennedy clan while undermining those who object to an all-green surface. These are only a few of the many groups and voices that have entered the debate. Some of the abutting owners have hired their own urban design consultants.

The Massachusetts Turnpike Authority controls the land, and last year it commissioned a $1 million study, led by Karen Alshuler of SMWM in San Francisco. The goal was to create a master plan—really a set of visual guidelines—under which landscape architects, yet to be selected, would develop designs for the various parcels. The Alshuler study operated within—and chose not to challenge—a set of rigid parcel-by-parcel constraints laid down more than a decade ago by the environmental permit (subsequently embodied in a special zoning law) that allowed the Big Dig to occur. These require that 75 percent of the land be "public open space," and in many cases they virtually dictate what can happen on each parcel. The authors of the study talked to everyone, in the vain hope of discovering consensus. As a result, they created a shallow, least-common-denominator document that lacks vision and invention and failed to ignite any enthusiasm. Many of the parcels are proposed to be simply grass plots with artfully angled paths.

Meanwhile, the state government, despite lengthy meetings and discussions, has failed to decide who will be responsible for managing and maintaining the land in the future. Presumably the city government will play some role in that, but nobody knows what.

It's a typical Boston brouhaha. Whatever happens, we can now be sure that the Big Dig will indeed get finished, at whatever financial cost. We can be sure, too, that Boston will be a better place for it. What is less certain is whether we will ever get beyond that, to seize the opportunity of a century to create a great and memorable example of city-making.

IV. Housing

Editor's Introduction

At the federal, state, and local levels, an array of city planners, politicians, architects, and developers are engaged in providing solutions to the nation's housing problems. The articles in this section treat some of the better-known housing issues, such as public housing, affordable homes, and mixed-income policies.

The first two articles cover recent changes in public housing, a term that refers to federally subsidized rental housing for low-income families, the elderly, and persons with disabilities. Public housing dates back to the 1930s and the Great Depression, when the United States government initiated a large-scale effort to create safe, decent housing for the poor. For many people today, the term calls to mind the large high-rise apartment complexes that went up in numerous cities during the urban renewal efforts of the 1950s and 1960s. The designers of these projects, inspired by the urban modernism of French architect Le Corbusier and his visions of a Radiant City based on simplicity and openness, built neighborhoods of uniform towers surrounded by grassy open spaces. They were originally intended to serve as subsidized housing for a combination of middle-class and low-income workers, but shifting demographics and economic restructuring tended to result in an influx of the poor and unemployed. After a drop in federal funding for public housing during the 1970s and 1980s, living conditions in many of these places deteriorated. The "projects," as they came to be known, eventually became synonymous with drugs and crime, poverty and despair.

During the past decade, however, a new trend has emerged in public housing: the blighted projects of the past are being torn down and replaced with attractive low-rise town houses, occupied by both low-income tenants paying subsidized rents and middle-class renters who pay market rates. These changes are largely the result of HOPE VI, a program launched in 1993 by the U.S. Department of Housing and Urban Development (HUD), which works to revitalize severely distressed public housing.

In "Tearing Down Years of Failure," Olivera Perkins discusses the redevelopment efforts underway at Longwood Apartments, a federally subsidized housing project in Cleveland, Ohio. Longwood, which first opened in 1957, has had a history marked by hopeful signs and discouraging failures, which Perkins recounts through the experiences of long-time residents. Longwood's $111 million redevelopment plan will include units for both low- and moderate-income tenants.

Ron Scherer, in "Public Housing Moves Toward Rich, Poor Together," examines the increased emphasis on providing mixed-income housing and the debate surrounding the issue. While advocates claim that mixed-income policies improve living conditions and make public housing more viable, critics contend that they ultimately hurt those at the bottom of the economic scale, who may find themselves forced out of their homes with no place else to go.

Another important concern for planners is making home-buying more affordable for lower-income families. Chris Palladino provides a detailed look at the creation of affordable housing in Fall Creek Place, an Indianapolis neighborhood, in his article, "If Revitalization Can Occur on the Near North Side of Indianapolis, It Can Occur Anywhere." Such developments are often a collaborative effort involving many different parties and funding from numerous sources.

In Fall Creek Place, the city used a $4 million grant from HUD and $10 million of its own funds to acquire the land and improve the infrastructure, and then secured private sector development expertise to oversee the construction and design elements. The new development offers a range of housing opportunities, and the city has arranged to provide lower-interest-rate mortgages, down-payment assistance, and property tax abatement for homebuyers, enabling a household that normally qualifies for a $100,000 home to afford a $140,000 home.

In his article "Affordable Housing: Who Pays Now?" James B. Goodno focuses on the subject of funding for housing developments. In particular, he discusses the increasing use of housing trust funds, which originated in the 1970s, to provide money for rental and down-payment assistance, as well as construction and rehabilitation costs. In 2002 Los Angeles created the nation's largest municipal affordable housing trust fund. Established with $42 million of the city's money, it is projected to grow to $100 million in three years, providing money for the creation and upkeep of about 4,000 to 5,000 units for low- and moderate-income city residents annually.

Tearing Down Years of Failure[1]

By Olivera Perkins
Plain Dealer, June 11, 2002

If you stand in the middle of Longwood Avenue, you can see the stark contrast between the past and the future of federally subsidized housing—both for Cleveland and the nation.

On the south side of the street are the remains of the aging, institutional-looking Longwood Apartments complex—low-rise buildings and garden apartments that are scattered throughout a roaming, 33-acre campus. On the north side you see neat rows of new townhouses, faced with brick and siding, that resemble many of the upscale subdivisions the city has used to woo suburbanites to Cleveland. The "new" Longwood has been renamed Arbor Park Village.

From Longwood Avenue, you also notice that city streets run through the new development. On the south side, big grassy areas separate the buildings.

When Longwood Apartments opened in 1957, those rambling green spaces were seen as progress. But by the late 1990s, proponents of demolishing Longwood said its open design was a major reason for its decline. Those unsecured parcels, they said, beckoned drug dealers to roam the area.

An unmistakable reminder of that came in February, when 40 men were caught in a major drug bust at the complex.

Police said one of the goals of the highly publicized bust was to set a line of demarcation between the old Longwood and the new. Residents aren't so sure that has happened.

"All they did is run them [drug dealers] away from one section to another," tenant Eddie Bradley said.

As the first Longwood tenants began moving across the street this month, longtime residents such as Bradley, Hattie James and Thelma Flowers say high hopes are tempered with skepticism brought on by the complex's long history of failure.

The struggles of Cleveland's first urban renewal project mirrored the often failing national effort to get the private sector to provide good, affordable housing for lower-income renters. Longwood became Cleveland's Cabrini-Green, the notorious Chicago public-housing project. Both began with a vision to save a neighborhood but became a symbol of what was destroying it.

---

1. From *The Plain Dealer* June 11, 2002. Copyright © 2002 *The Plain Dealer*. All rights reserved. Reprinted with permission.

Today, Longwood again finds itself part of a national trend to reinvent publicly subsidized housing by dramatically renovating complexes and sometimes demolishing and rebuilding developments that have had a long history of failure.

The first phase of the $111 million Arbor Park Village development—282 units expected to be completed by November—officially opened June 3. It is being built on land where the first of the old apartments were torn down. As Arbor Park fills up, the rest of Longwood will be leveled.

By 2005, the 629 units will completely replace the current sprawling complex, which is off Woodland Avenue, roughly between East 35th and East 40th streets, close enough to downtown to see the city skyline.

Flowers, who already has moved in, was on the committee that chose the new name.

"I wanted a name that would say that Longwood was gone," she said. Arbor Park "sounded high-class. I wanted to live like that."

James, also among the first to make the move, wants Arbor Park Village to fulfill all of Longwood's broken promises. Yet after having spent more than 30 years at that complex, she is haunted by its history.

"They always said they were going to make it better," James said. "They ended up making it worse."

Criticism Started Early

The section of Cleveland's Central neighborhood where Longwood is located used to be called Area B. In 1950s Cleveland, the neighborhood was a vivid metaphor for blight, decay and deferred dreams.

Area B was teeming with newly arrived black Southerners who lived in rundown houses, most of them owned by suburban landlords. The tuberculosis rate was six times the city average and the infant mortality rate twice the average.

But renting was profitable. Landlords collected as much as $1,000 a month by subdividing large houses and leasing them to several families. In 1950, only about 15 percent of renters in Greater Cleveland paid more than $60 for rental units.

Cleveland passed a $7 million bond in 1953, to take advantage of federal urban renewal incentives to cities that bought and demolished property in blighted areas. The goal was to redevelop Area B as housing for working-class families.

However, about a year before the first Longwood buildings opened, the designs were panned by a committee of architects and artists. "Don't use these as a model for future urban renewal," the committee members said in a 1956 *Plain Dealer* article.

The committee blasted the apartments for having dull exteriors and small rooms—the same complaints that were being made 40 years later.

By 1960, Longwood's owner, the Cleveland Development Foundation, said the bank was threatening to foreclose. Foundation officials said they missed mortgage payments because of high vacancies and tenants who couldn't afford the rent.

Longwood was intended for black residents, trapped there by segregation. But by the late 1950s, when whites began leaving Cleveland for the suburbs, new areas of the city were being opened to blacks. The same thing was happening in other urban centers around the country.

"The people with reasonably stable incomes that they thought would have lived in these urban renewal developments ended up leaving," said Cushing Dolbeare, a Harvard scholar who has studied urban housing trends for 50 years.

As they did, problems ensued.

Relief, Then More Problems

In 1961, Congress passed the "Longwood Amendment," aimed at increasing the monthly cash flow to nonprofit owners by allowing them to refinance at lower rates, with fewer fees and with much lower minimum payments.

Two years later, the complex's owners refinanced.

For a time, the changes seemed to help.

Thelma Flowers and her three children moved to Longwood in 1965. The screening process was thorough, the rules plentiful.

"And there was grass!" Flowers said.

For her that meant management cared enough to keep up the grounds, and residents had pride enough not to destroy where they lived.

Hattie James and her three children moved to the complex in 1970 because she believed tenants shared her values.

"Most people worked," said James, a retired hospital worker. "They took their kids to the playground. They planted pretty flowers."

But by the early 1970s, many nonprofits were threatening to get out of the low-income housing business because they said federal subsidies weren't keeping up with inflation, especially escalating energy costs. In 1974, the Nixon administration and Congress created a plan for generous, long-term federal subsidies to private landlords.

The subsidies didn't help Longwood.

In 1976, tenants took control of Longwood by forming a cooperative that was owned by the residents, governed by an elected board and managed by a private firm. Tenant leaders promised a well-maintained complex, job training and placement and other programs that would help residents into the middle class.

It never happened. In 1982, the U.S. Department of Housing and Urban Development cited Longwood's management firm for several questionable practices, including making improper payments to maintenance contractors. In 1986, HUD seized control of the complex as the owners were $13 million in debt despite a $2 million annual subsidy.

> ***One day I looked up and nobody moving in had a job."***—C. M. Hope, Longwood, OH, resident

In 1987, Associated Estates Realty Corp. bought the complex, with an even more generous federal subsidy.

The first few years were good. The owner even received high marks from Washington for turning Longwood around.

Then history began to repeat itself.

"They [Associated Estates] told us that they were going to renovate the property," tenant Thelma Flowers said. "All they did was put a little carpet on the floor, and a little paint on the walls. That was probably the last time they did anything."

Seeking an Answer

By the early 1990s, crime was increasing and property deteriorating so rapidly that tenants who had lived in Longwood for years moved.

Tenant C. M. Hope, who has lived there more than 30 years, said the newcomers were different. For decades, most residents were working-class people.

"Then one day I looked up and nobody moving in had a job," she said. "They were letting these young girls with babies—I mean teenagers—in here. They began bringing their friends. I think that is when all the drugs and crime started happening."

Longwood became a drug dealer's paradise. Close to downtown and exits for Interstates 77, 90 and 490, dealers had their pick of a suburban and local clientele.

In late 1998, a 17-year-old was killed in a turf war between rival gangs seeking control of the neighborhood drug trade. The killing capped a rash of violent acts among feuding gangs.

As the troubles mounted, HUD forced Associated Estates to relinquish ownership of the complex in 1999 because of years of mismanagement.

Associated Estates says it was not to blame for the problems and never received credit for investing in the area.

"Regrettably, the management challenges grew beyond traditional methods due to social ills not unlike those that afflict other dense central city properties with subsidies," the company said in a statement released last week.

With Associated Estates gone, the question remained: What next?

Initially, HUD proposed demolishing the complex and giving tenants Section 8 vouchers, said Michael Foley, executive director of the Cleveland Tenants Organization. His group opposed vouchers because it doubted the market could absorb a flood of more than 700 families.

Council President Frank Jackson, who represents the Central neighborhood, said he and tenants believed HUD had an obligation to make Longwood work.

As early as 1997, a committee of Longwood tenants and public officials began putting pressure on HUD to find a buyer committed to building a new complex. In 1999, the Finch Group of Boston, which has a track record for improving distressed housing, bought Longwood.

Jackson said finding a buyer was tough, but not as hard as pulling together $111 million of mostly public money. "We kept getting from people the 'why nots' about why a new Longwood would not work," he said.

Not Just New Buildings

With the money finally in place, the first bulldozers arrived last summer.

Robert James Jr., Finch's executive vice president, said rebuilding Longwood is more than a bricks-and-mortar issue.

Arbor Park Village will have a variety of programs, including educational and social activities for children and resources to help adults get better jobs.

Finch's James said the complex also wants to attract tenants with moderate incomes. Almost 90 percent of Longwood's tenants had incomes of less than $10,000 a year. Under federal guidelines, Arbor Park will be able to rent to a family of four with an income as high as $48,000.

But luring those families to the complex isn't easy.

Lakesha Paris had to do some strong convincing to get her husband, Darnell Paris, to even look at a model at Arbor Park Village.

"When she said Longwood, my impression was, 'No, no, no!'" he said. "When I came here and saw it, I could hardly believe it."

Cushing Dolbeare, the housing analyst, said mixed-income developments are more desirable than ones with a high concentration of very poor residents. But they also raise questions. Where will the very poor tenants end up finding housing? Is a mixed-income development more vulnerable for gentrification?

Foley of the Cleveland Tenants Organization said all that is happening makes him optimistic about Longwood's—or Arbor Park's—future.

Larry and Sharon Sanders, tenants for 14 years, said it is too early to be optimistic.

"We're going to sit back and see what it is going to be like," Larry Sanders said. "We would like to see that it works, but you know the track record isn't too good."

Public Housing Moves Toward Rich, Poor Together[2]

By Ron Scherer
The Christian Science Monitor, February 8, 1999

With its rooftop pool and health club, the Metropolitan is one of the most sought after addresses in Bethesda, Md. Two-bedroom apartments rent for up to $2,000 per month, and at least one couple rents a separate apartment for their children and nanny. But, interspersed throughout the high rise are apartments that rent for as little as $288 per month.

For the families on public assistance in these apartments, the concept of a nanny is as remote as season tickets to the opera.

This blending of incomes at the Metropolitan, which is owned by a public housing authority, is symbolic of some of the biggest changes sweeping public housing in 30 years. Those changes range from a historic shift to mixed-income housing to a measure allowing public-housing tenants to have pets. Many have been under way for some time, but they will continue to accelerate, due to a housing reform bill quietly passed by Congress last fall.

"In the 21st century, the processes we used 50 years ago may not work the way they were intended—the bill provides incentives so we can manage it better," says Harold Lucas, an assistant secretary at the Department of Housing and Urban Development (HUD).

Income mixing is likely to prove the most far-reaching aspect of the bill, experts say. In the past, federal law mandated that preference for housing go to the poorest of the poor—households making 30 percent or less of median income. But under the new law, public-housing authorities will be permitted to "skip" over families. So someone with a higher income could get into public housing sooner than someone with a lower income.

"This bill has the potential to dramatically change who is served by housing-assistance dollars," says Linda Couch of the National Low Income Housing Coalition in Washington. Experts estimate up to 80 percent of the nation's 3,400 public housing authorities could be affected.

The change to mixed-income housing began a few years ago, and was sparked by a desire to move away from the giant high-rises of the 1970s and give public-housing recipients safer, cleaner places to live.

"When you have people leaving for work with their lunch boxes or attache cases, it provides a role model," says Hilly Gross, a spokesman for the New York City Housing Authority, which mandates that 1 of every 2 new renters have a job.

For example, under the "Hope VI" program, which replaces dilapidated housing, all new public housing must include income mixing and low-rise, garden-type apartments. "If you research from the old days, we were always on the wrong side of the tracks—too dense, too tall, always harboring the poorest of the poor, and we generally had a hard time sustaining how the public housing program should run," says Mr. Lucas. Now, he says, the new units will house the moderately poor and the working poor, as well as welfare recipients.

This prospect concerns some advocates for the poor. They argue that the bottom rung is getting squeezed out. "This could be destabilizing for poor people and their quality of life," argues David Jones, the president of the Community Service Society (CSS) of New York.

In fact, the St. Paul, Minn., Public Housing Agency has rejected the concept of mixed-income housing for the 20,000 people it serves. Helping those who need it most "is a reflection of the core values of this inner city," says John Gutzmann, executive director.

Under the "Hope VI" program, all new public housing must include income mixing and low-rise, garden-type apartments.

Other public-housing officials, however, believe mixing incomes has a lot of benefits, including in nonhousing areas such as schools, libraries, and hospitals. "My wife is a school teacher, and I can tell you that with mixed-income housing you have no schools with a high concentration of low-income children, you don't have pockets of poverty," says Roy Appletree, assistant executive director of the Montgomery County Housing Opportunities Commission in Maryland.

To avoid dislocating people, the new law provides 50,000 new vouchers for families eligible for subsidized housing. And the shift in residents won't happen overnight, because the vacancy rate in public housing is relatively low. Ms. Couch says it will take five years to evaluate the effects of the change.

For many public-housing authorities, there will be a much faster impact as a result of another new change, which encourages the housing authorities to become more entrepreneurial.

In the past, any non-rent income a public housing authority earned had to be returned to HUD, discouraging managers from seeking out commercial tenants. Under the new law, the housing authority will get to keep the money.

One of the strongest advocates of the change is Richard Leco, executive director of the Central Falls Housing Authority in Rhode Island. "We're trying to get our residents to be self-sufficient, so we should be self-sufficient as well," he argues. Mr. Leco, for example, leases the rooftops of his public housing units to cell phone companies. He uses the income to pay employees working in nonprofit reading programs and computer labs.

One of his most recent efforts is training tenants as interns at his organization, in hopes they can get jobs as temps at other housing authorities. In the future, he envisions renting out space for a doughnut kiosk or hair salon. "I have a 10-story building with awnings, I could sell advertising space," he says.

The entrepreneurial spirit is also spreading to the giant New York authority, which houses more than 600,000 people. The city is negotiating with satellite television companies to rent out roof space in a deal that could earn $350,000 to $360,000 per year. In addition, Mr. Gross says the commercial possibilities open up training opportunities. "If a vending machine company . . . wants to put machines in our buildings, they have to agree to train our tenants."

That speaks to a major concern of community activists: "Will the money go back to the tenants living there?" asks Mr. Jones of CSS. "Will they get the benefits?"

If Revitalization Can Occur on the Near North Side of Indianapolis, It Can Occur Anywhere[3]

By Chris Palladino
PLANNING, March 2003

A victim of urban renewal, this 26-block neighborhood lost nearly 80 percent of its housing stock between 1956 and 1999. For many years, the area was called "Dodge City."

Then, in 1997, the city received a $4 million Homeownership Zone grant from the U.S. Department of Housing and Urban Development. Indianapolis was one of 12 cities nationwide to receive this grant, which was earmarked for construction of affordable, private housing in blighted urban neighborhoods.

U.S. Rep. Julia Carson, a long-time resident of the neighborhood who helped secure the grant, says, "Too many years of neglect and decline, of flight and fight, left the neighborhood in dire straits. Now an ingenious recipe is bringing life and livability back, providing a model not only for other cities but also for the future redevelopment of our own diverse communities."

Getting Started

Upon receipt of the federal grant, the city embarked on a one-year planning and urban design process. What ultimately resulted was a name (Fall Creek Place) and a mission statement: to transform a blighted inner-city neighborhood into a healthy, mixed-income, diverse community providing a range of housing opportunities, recreational amenities, and commercial support services.

Now, six years later, the project has received APA's Current Topic Award for implementing smart growth.

Fall Creek Place covers more than 26 city blocks. While the original HUD grant calls for 265 homes, more than 300 developable home sites have been identified, as well as 46 rehabilitations. Other components of the original master plan include strengthening retail nodes, adding neighborhood parks, providing new gateways, and making significant infrastructure improvements.

Construction began last year, and phase one is under way, with 81 housing units already built or renovated and an additional 92 units under construction. Phase two home construction began in the summer of 2002, and phase three homes will likely begin construction this spring.

Part of the success of Fall Creek Place stems from the strong public support received during the planning process, says Jennifer Green, project manager for the city of Indianapolis. The combination of strong public buy-in and full support from the mayor's office allowed Fall Creek Place to move forward. It was important that this development not be seen as a broad-based gentrification effort that would displace existing residents. "Our commitment was that the city would not buy out any existing owner-occupied unit within the project boundaries," notes Green.

As part of its commitment to building a mixed community, HUD required the city to pledge that 51 percent of new housing units would go to households earning 80 percent or less of the city's area median income.

Calling on Private Developers

Early on, the city realized an important element was missing: private sector development expertise. Through a competitive procurement process, Mansur Real Estate Services, Inc., a local company specializing in urban development, was selected as master developer in the summer of 2000. Mansur requested six months to prepare an implementation strategy.

"The master plan was a great start," says Charles Cagann, Mansur's president, "but it didn't delve into what resources it would take to turn that vision into a reality. We needed time to craft a realistic implementation strategy that would serve as the blueprint for moving Fall Creek Place forward."

Mansur's 89-page strategy emphasized six key areas: infrastructure, housing design, financial resources, project phasing, marketing strategy, and builder program. "Looking back, it was the implementation strategy that made this development successful," says Carolyn Coleman, deputy mayor. "The city understood exactly what it would take, including financial resources, to bring the project to fruition. Preparing it was a far more intensive effort than the master planning process."

The city's involvement in Fall Creek Place came at the front end. Subsidies and incentives were needed to ensure the desired mix of low- and moderate-income and market-rate buyers. But equally important was for the developer and builders to incur some level of risk. Using a master developer to structure the overall program allowed the city to accomplish this goal.

Many urban housing developments led by community development corporations use a contractor, with a set payment schedule from the CDC. At Fall Creek Place, home builders buy home sites with their own funds, assume a construction loan, and finance the construction themselves before selling to the end buyer. The collaborative marketing program and a subordination program on lot purchases helped minimize the overall risk.

"In many respects, Fall Creek Place is structured exactly like a conventional residential subdivision," notes Cagann. "It simply needed the city's upfront commitment of resources to overcome the obstacles inherent in any urban development."

Eight charter builders have participated in Fall Creek Place, representing a mix of larger, production builders and smaller, low-volume custom homebuilders. Four of the eight building firms are owned by women, and one is minority-owned. To help level the playing field between the larger and smaller builders, each builder was given funding to construct one model home and one speculative home for a home show last June. Each builder could subordinate three home sites, thus allowing smaller builders to build without having to secure capital for the land at the beginning.

"Coopera-tion and collabora-tion embodies this neigh-borhood's can-do spirit."— **Mayor Bart Peterson, IN**

"The cooperation and collaboration of project partners, from both the private and public sectors, embodies this neighborhood's can-do spirit and is evident by what we see here today. Because of the dedication of these partnerships, Fall Creek Place has the potential to serve as a redevelopment model for communities across the nation," says Mayor Bart Peterson, himself a former real estate developer.

The City's Commitment

The city's original $4 million HUD grant was used almost exclusively for property acquisition and relocation of residents who had been living in rental housing. In 2001, the city committed $10 million to finance infrastructure improvements, which included new streets, curbs, sidewalks, alleys, street lighting, landscaping, and entry features.

The city also committed Community Development Block Grant and HOME funds for down payment assistance to qualified homebuyers. Finally, the city provided a guarantee of a "buildable home site" by paying the costs of removing subsurface debris from the basements of demolished housing units.

As part of the city's infrastructure program, a sewer tap, water lateral, and a water meter pit were provided for each property, further lowering the builder's costs and keeping housing prices affordable.

Fall Creek Place homebuyers were offered a variety of financial incentives. Six local banks agreed to offer discounted mortgages, at an average rate of one percent below conventional standard rates. In phase one only, market rate homebuyers could receive up to $10,000 of matching down payment assistance. For all phases, low-

and moderate-income homebuyers are eligible for up to $24,000 in down payment assistance on a sliding scale based on income levels and household size.

All down payment assistance is structured as a "soft second" mortgage fully dissolved after five to 10 years, depending on the size of the grant. Buyers who sell their home before then must repay a portion of the grant award. Finally, the city provided a five-year residential tax abatement to all homebuyers who bought their property before the end of 2002. That amounts to an annual savings of about $1,300.

With the combination of lower interest rate mortgages, down payment assistance, and property tax abatement, a household that normally qualifies for a $100,000 home can afford a $140,000 home. Conversely, the pool of eligible applicants who can afford a $100,000 home has been greatly expanded.

Unlike many affordable housing programs, what sets Fall Creek Place apart is the unusual array of choices offered to low- and moderate-income buyers. Buyers pick their own builder, their own home plans, and their home site. And having eight builders gives all buyers the ability to compare and contrast.

Design Issues

One of the greatest challenges was balancing affordability with quality design. But project team members wanted the new housing to adhere to design standards—and for units occupied by low- and moderate-income households to be indistinguishable from market-rate units.

The development team created design guidelines to ensure compatibility. With the cooperation of the city, a design review committee now reviews all home plans in Fall Creek Place, and all plans within the area's boundaries must get a special stamp from the committee before receiving a city building permit. Members of the review committee include representatives of Mansur, the city, and Rottmann Architects of Indianapolis, the project architect.

Besides issuing written guidelines, the project team hired Rottmann Architects to design five prototype single-family detached houses and one townhouse. These prototype drawings were offered to all eight charter builders. In addition, the builders may provide their own designs, as long as they adhere to the design guidelines. The guidelines focus on scale, proportions, orientation, and key elevation features.

Moving Forward

Construction of the model homes began with a ceremonial groundbreaking in July 2001. The initial market study called for 40 units to be sold in the first year. In the first 12 months, contracts were in hand for more than 200 new homes.

Phase one and phase two infrastructure improvements were substantially complete by the end of 2002 (one year ahead of schedule), allowing 250 homes to be under construction by this spring and summer. As of this January, 60 new homes and 21 rehabilitations had been completed and sold to homebuyers. Another 92 units are under construction, and another 11 rehabs are in

It seems that Fall Creek Place may fall victim to its own success.

progress. Projections show an average of 10 to 20 new units a month starting construction over the next year.

As planned, half the units are market rate and half are for low- and moderate-income families. Median sale prices were $132,000 in phase one and are $125,000 in phase two. Homes have been sold for as low as $94,000 and as high as $250,000. Higher appraisals are common in Fall Creek Place. On average, final appraisals for new homes are approximately 15 percent higher than the sale prices.

In June 2002, the Builders' Association of Greater Indianapolis included Fall Creek Place in its annual Parade of Homes, one of the region's largest home shows. This was the first year that the Builder's Association included an urban development as part of the event. Eight homes were opened to the public, and nearly 9,000 people toured the homes over four days.

The next challenge for Fall Creek Place is to meet demand for housing in the community. Since last July, when all phase two home sites were officially filled, more than 500 inquiries have been received. Common requests include start-up dates for phase three and possible expansion of the project boundaries.

At this point, it seems that Fall Creek Place may fall victim to its own success. Vacant properties that the city could have acquired several years ago have now escalated in value, and owners are less inclined to sell. When costs are added to cover debris removal, utility connections, and related soft costs, the total improved lot basis adds up to more than $30,000, without even factoring in the city's public infrastructure improvements. All of these factors make affordable housing a more difficult goal to achieve without continued subsidies.

Still, the city remains optimistic about what may happen next. "Future opportunities for Fall Creek Place are limitless," says Mayor Peterson, "as home construction and rehabilitation will lay the foundation for a dynamic blend of families that will continue to enrich this unique neighborhood."

Affordable Housing: Who Pays Now?[4]

By James B. Goodno
Planning, November 2002

Jan Breidenbach knows what it takes to build affordable housing. "You need dirt, you need financing, and you need political will," says the director of the Southern California Association of Non-Profit Housing.

The formula sounds simple, but in Los Angeles, it has been nearly impossible to put the three together.

"No units are available," adds Jane Blumenfeld, director of city-wide planning for Los Angeles. But the city is moving forward. Housing advocates have developed a sophisticated political strategy that is transforming the nation's second-largest city into a leader in affordable housing policy.

In May, Los Angeles created the nation's largest municipal affordable housing trust fund. Launched with $42 million of the city's money, the fund will grow to $100 million in three years and help finance the construction and rehabilitation of an estimated 4,000 to 5,000 units for low- and moderate-income residents annually.

In addition, the city is reforming land-use policy to remove obstacles to housing production. The city's new comprehensive plan calls for mixed-use development along hundreds of miles of boulevards, and the planning department has drawn up a set of zoning and permitting changes that Blumenfeld hopes will encourage developers to build more affordable units.

These achievements haven't occurred in a political vacuum. "On their own, the housing groups couldn't get a housing trust fund through the city council and past the mayor, no matter how bad the situation," says Peter Dreier, co-director of the Urban and Environmental Policy Institute at Occidental College in Los Angeles and former head of the Boston Redevelopment Authority. "We made a calculated decision to get organized labor and the religious community involved and to neutralize or engage the business community."

Taking Stock

From Florida to Silicon Valley, creating broad support for investment, changing land-use policies, and finding the land all are moving affordable housing policy forward. Employers, developers, unions, and religious leaders have joined together in aggressive campaigns.

Local efforts are tied to a drop in federal funding since the late 1970s and a concurrent rise in demand. While the problem affects middle-income people in many places, it is particularly acute for households earning less that 30 percent of the local median income. The Millennial Housing Commission, a panel established by Congress to study the nation's housing situation, says it will take 250,000 new units a year for 20 years to house these poorest Americans.

The shortage of units—estimated at more than 4 million in the mid-1990s—is not evenly distributed. The gap between supply and demand is greatest in regions with the highest cost of living. In Massachusetts, the "least affordable state" according to the National Low-Income Housing Coalition, the Boston janitors union (Service Employees Local 254) has made a major issue of the gap between wages and rents. In Florida, workers live in inland counties and work on the coast. And in California's Silicon Valley, despite a precipitous downturn in the local economy, housing remains out of reach for many families.

The problem is not limited to the boomtowns and growth centers of the 1990s. "There's a disparity between the cost of housing and what folks earn here, principally in inner city and rural parts of

---

"There's a disparity between the cost of housing and what folks earn here."—Jim Cain, Iowa Coalition for Housing and the Homeless

---

the state," says Jim Cain, executive director of the Iowa Coalition for Housing and the Homeless. "The University of Iowa did a study on housing needs in 2000, and one of the findings was that 68 out of 99 Iowa counties had stagnant or declining markets."

With home values so low, Cain adds, "it's difficult to develop affordable housing in those counties because the appraised value won't be as high as the cost of the new or rehabbed home."

Local Resources

Trust funds have become a popular tool for obtaining funding on a continuing basis. "There are at least 175 housing trust funds in different cities, counties, and states," says Mary Brooks, director of the housing trust fund project at the Center for Community Change, a national group that provides technical assistance to organizations in low-income communities. "At any given time 20 to 30 places are thinking about housing trust funds, and that estimate is probably conservative."

First created in the late 1970s, trust funds multiplied in the 1990s, thanks in part to changes in the laws of New Jersey, Pennsylvania, and other states that encouraged local financing. They support an array of activities, including rental and down-payment assistance. Most support at least some new construction or rehabilitation activities.

While trust funds have been gaining popularity in recent years, the size of the Los Angeles fund and the city's perseverance have drawn considerable attention.

"I was surprised we got it through post-September 11," admits Eric Garcetti, a housing advocate and city council member. "We were looking at a quarter-of-a-million-dollar deficit—the largest in our history—then we hit 9/11, and I didn't think housing would be a high priority for many council members. The mayor was really wonderful. He kept saying, 'This is the right thing to do.'"

"Mayor [James] Hahn really comes at this from two points," explains Deputy Mayor Jonathon Kevles. "As city attorney, he had experiences walking through slum housing, seeing the conditions, convicting landlords for violations. Second, he sees it as an economic development issue. It becomes difficult to attract people when 70 percent can't afford to buy a house or find it hard to rent."

Ideally, trust funds receive revenues from dedicated sources such as development fees and taxes. That there are no fixed methods for capitalizing trust funds is shown in California's Santa Clara County, where popular desire to address Silicon Valley's housing crisis was matched by resistance to higher taxes.

"Our fund is somewhat novel," says Laura Stuchinsky, housing director for the Silicon Valley Manufacturers Group, an alliance of 190 high-tech companies. "This one undertook a two-year campaign to raise $20 million to capitalize it." Two-thirds of the money ended up coming from private donations, the county kicked in $2 million, and the cities gave the remainder. The Santa Clara Housing Trust Fund may prove particularly beneficial to smaller cities, such as Cupertino, a suburb with 52,000 residents, which contributed $250,000 in hopes of leveraging more than the city can raise on its own.

Although the city of Los Angeles decided to finance its fund, there is no dedicated revenue source. Housing advocates agreed to take linkage fees and inclusionary zoning off the table in order to satisfy business and developer interests. To work out financial and other details, the city created a task force headed by Mike Feuer, a former member of the city council. The focus, Feuer says, is funding sources, administration, and the sticky issue of targeting beneficiaries.

"There are good public policy reasons to identify the poorest residents of Los Angeles as the target, and we know that $100 million, even with leveraging, won't be enough to meet the needs of L.A.'s poorest," Feuer says. "But there are also good public policy reasons to target better off residents—the firefighters and schoolteachers—who are not among the poorest but who can't afford to buy a house without a subsidy." Housing advocates believe the bulk of the money should go for the very poor, but they have agreed that some funds should be used for moderate-income workers, especially public employees.

Sunshine State

While Los Angeles is just beginning, Florida has used trust funds for a decade.

"Our comprehensive planning process includes a housing mandate that says cities and counties must house all current and expected residents," says Jamie Ross, housing director for 1,000 Friends of Florida and president of the Florida Housing Coalition. "Local governments don't like unfunded mandates, and this was unfunded until 1992, until we enacted the Sadowski Affordable Housing Act."

The Sadowski Act increased the documentary stamp fee on real estate transactions by 10 cents per $100 and dedicated 70 percent of that to cities and counties. SHIP—the State Housing Initiative Policy Program—delivers the local aid. For fiscal year 2002–2003, the Sadowski Act will generate close to $250 million, $175 million for local governments. The act also created the Catalyst Program, which receives $350,000 a year to provide technical assistance and training to local governments and housing nonprofits.

The city of Tallahassee makes use of SHIP funds, CDBG and HOME grants, and its own trust fund to support affordable housing initiatives. While the city does some multi-family rental housing programs, it focuses on ownership assistance for low- and moderate-income households, offering down payment assistance loans to about 75 home buyers a year, says Martha Bentley, a housing specialist in the city's neighborhood services office.

"We set up our housing trust fund in 1992, we saw a need in the community, and we set aside the original amount of $2.2 million," says city commissioner Debbie Lightsey. "We set it up so most of the money would be revolving funds with some grants. The balance is down to $1.2 million, but it took 10 years to get there, and we think we can keep the fund going." Development fees on projects without affordable housing are expected to help refinance the trust.

The trust fund's flexibility is a valuable tool in working with nonprofit developers. "Trust funds don't have the same strings as federal and state money," says Lightsey, "Habitat for Humanity is very active here, but its money comes irregularly, and it needed money up front. We extended a $100,000 line of credit at one percent interest that it can draw from. Habitat pays back the loan when their money comes in. This smooth flow of money allowed them to double their construction."

This is not unique to Tallahassee. Chris Block, executive director of Charities Housing, the development arm of Catholic Charities in California's Silicon Valley, says this is also an important attribute of the Santa Clara County Housing Trust Fund. "In our real estate market, it's hard to compete," he says. "You have to be able to access land as quickly as possible. Getting gap financing allows us to move quickly and makes other financing possible."

Financing is only one part of Tallahassee's effort. The city continues to address an interwoven set of land-use, zoning, and revitalization issues, including crime, business development, and education.

"We want to infuse affordable housing throughout the community," says commissioner Lightsey. "We are struggling with the idea of urban sprawl," adds Martha Bentley, "so we have concentrated our CHDO (Community Housing Development Organizations) development in infill housing. Our aim is to take neighborhoods that need revitalization and build them up with home ownership."

Tallahassee also is working on incentives for developers, city planning director Wendy Gray says. "We authorized the development review committee to grant deviations upon request for most development standards as long as they are not environmental standards—for example, setbacks. We've included a density bonus of up to 25 percent, we've allowed any kind of building, for example, duplex, triplex for inclusive units—the unit might appear to be single family from the front—where code would normally prohibit that. For developments below a certain size we'll offer a full waiver for development fees."

Los Angeles has been addressing similar issues since creating a comprehensive plan two years ago that allows mixed-use development with 108 housing units per acre on major commercial corridors. Planners have proposed a series of reforms to make development on the corridors more feasible by reducing the need for height and setback variances, for example. This would be good for neighborhoods where there is "way too much commercial zoning and not enough housing," Jane Blumenfeld says.

The planning department has also proposed a by-right density bonus of 35 percent for projects that meet affordability and transit requirements, and elimination of density formulas that discourage large-family units in multifamily housing.

Design Matters, But It's Not Everything

Even with housing-friendly policies in place, Los Angeles faces intense land-use squabbles as developers and planners identify affordable housing sites.

"We've had to engage the community, to change the stereotype of affordable housing," says Robin Hughes, executive director of the Los Angeles Community Design Center, a nonprofit development, planning, and architecture firm. Hughes notes resistance from homeowners concerned about property values and residents of low-income neighborhoods upset by the "dumping" of housing projects in their midst. "We have to educate neighbors on who we are, on long-term project impact on the neighborhood, on our belief in good design, and on solid property management," Hughes says.

Mike Pyatok, an Oakland architect who specializes in affordable housing, believes designers can move affordable housing forward by having communities envision their future. He encourages a hands-on approach in which potential tenants and other residents are invited to participate in the design and planning. The resulting buy-in, he says, can help move a project through the public planning process.

In Silicon Valley, good design is almost mandatory if a project is to move forward. "People have an image of affordable housing that has nothing to do with reality," says city council member Sandy James. She shows off good projects, finds the resources to help developers improve their design, and takes a proactive approach to development and planning. "We like to sit down early with developers, to talk about our vision, before plans are drawn," James says. "This way, we tend to get good projects with early buy in on what the community wants."

James took the initiative in getting the Santa Clara County Housing Trust Fund to join with Prometheus Development, a for-profit developer of multifamily market-rate housing, to offer a $10,000 award for affordable design.

"People have an image of affordable housing that has nothing to do with reality."—Sandy James, city council member

---

"We wanted to showcase that good design in affordable housing doesn't have to cost more," says Jackie Safier, a Prometheus partner. "The winner was a project in downtown Palo Alto, one of the most expensive places to live in the country."

Alma Place, a single-room occupancy project completed in 1998, won the initial prize. Built by the Palo Alto Housing Corporation, its 106 units are affordable to people earning no more than a third of the area median income. It is situated on a half-acre site within walking distance of jobs, stores, services, and transportation. The developer and designers Rob Wellington Quigley and Ron Wigginton won praise for using smart-growth principles, light-enhancing bay windows, efficient landscaping, and high ceilings. "It was a very simple, but elegant and well-thought-out design," Safier says.

San Jose's Progress

San Jose, with close to 1 million people, is the largest city in Silicon Valley. It has undergone tremendous change in recent years. The epicenter of the most recent economic boom, San Jose has worked to recreate its downtown, improve transportation, and address housing shortages at virtually all income levels.

When Ron Gonzales became mayor in 1999, "he challenged the city to double housing production," says David Vossbrink, his communications director. "We held monthly meetings with high-level commitment, with the city council, with developers, and we are on track to create an average of 1,200 affordable homes per year."

Since 1998, San Jose has achieved substantial success by earmarking more than $239 million in gap financing that has produced more than 5,400 new affordable homes throughout the city. That money helped leverage $877 million from other sources.

In September, the city council dedicated an additional $544 million from the city and its redevelopment agency to housing over the next five years. Officials hope this will leverage an additional $1.6 billion from other governmental and private entities.

Building on Success

Adopting good policies and finding funding sources are steps in a long, continuing process. Deciding where affordable housing is located, often on a regional basis, is one of the next challenges.

"Suburbs haven't viewed affordable housing as a benefit."—**Tim Shanahan, housing task force coordinator for United Way's Human Services Planning Alliance, Polk County, Iowa**

"Suburbs haven't viewed affordable housing as a benefit," says Tim Shanahan, housing task force coordinator for United Way's Human Services Planning Alliance in Polk County, Iowa. "That's where the new jobs are being created and where there is great need for affordable housing. Right now there are no requirements that developers include affordable units in their projects."

Tallahassee is working on adding inclusionary zoning to its toolbox. "In our 1996–97 evaluations, we discovered the issue was not just the amount of housing, but where the housing was located," says planning director Wendy Gray. "Demographic analysis showed the county was becoming more segregated."

In Los Angeles, advocates and developers say, you must pay attention to streamlining procedures and helping developers find the right combination of local, state, federal, and private financing.

"I would hope that now that we have the housing trust fund, the housing department can establish a systematic plan for allocating money," says Robin Hughes of the Los Angeles Design Center. "Now that they know they have $42 million to $100 million available, perhaps they can create schedules and add more predictability to the funding cycle."

Despite these concerns, and hoping for more federal money, many housing advocates and developers feel upbeat. "I'm more encouraged about affordable housing than I have ever been," says Silicon Valley's Chris Block.

Pointing to an aggressive campaign to approve a California housing bond at the polls in November, and the "energetic effort" behind the national trust fund campaign, Block adds that "if they all come together, we're going to make a real run at solving this problem."

Feds Must Do More, Housing Advocates Say

Advocates of a national housing trust fund want to get the federal government back in the business of seriously financing affordable housing construction and rehabilitation. That's because they believe it will require a concerted national effort to address the nation's housing problems.

"Financing affordable housing is ultimately a federal responsibility," says Peter Dreier, co-director of the Urban and Environmental Policy Institute at Occidental College in Los Angeles.

The federal government does not disagree. Representatives of the U.S. Department of Housing and Urban Development acknowledge the need for increased spending on affordable housing, but question some of the methods proposed by advocates for financing a trust fund. Meanwhile, the Millennial Housing Commission has called for an expanded federal role.

"Addressing this problem will require concerted efforts both to expand the supply of rental housing and to preserve the existing stock of subsidized and unsubsidized low-cost housing," the commission declared in its final report in May. "The addition of 150,000 units annually would make substantial progress toward meeting the housing needs of [extremely low-income] households, but it would take annual production of more than 250,000 units for more than 20 years to close the gap."

More Resources and Tools Needed

Because state and local governments and the private sector do not have the capacity to produce enough housing units, commissioners believe the federal government must expand the available resources and tools. The government has not entirely abandoned production. The HOME investment partnership program provides direct assistance for housing programs designed and administered at the state or local level. Community development block grants allow cities and counties to finance affordable housing and other local initiatives.

In its proposed budget of $31.5 billion for fiscal 2003, HUD asked Congress for $2.1 billion for HOME program, $238 million more than 2002, and $4,436 billion for CDBG, an increase of $95 million. HUD also has worked with local housing authorities to redevelop failed housing projects through its HOPE VI program. Although HOPE VI has been praised for its design and social impact, its emphasis on mixed-income housing and elimination of the unit-for-unit replacement mandate has led to a decline in the number of units, especially those for very low-income renters.

Changing Priorities, an annual report by the National Low-Income Housing Coalition, says that between 1976 and 2000, federal housing assistance budget authority dropped 51 percent, from $51.2 billion to $18.5 billion in inflation-adjusted dollars. "Almost all of the 1976 budget authority was spent on expanding the stock of assisted housing through production, rehabilitation, and rental assistance, whereas in 1999 most of it was spent on maintaining or improving the existing stock of housing assistance and renewing expiring subsidy contracts," the report says.

"The commitment to solving serious housing problems has all but vanished," says Sheila Crowley, president of the National Low-Income Housing Coalition. "Beginning at the end of the 1970s," Crowley says, "the federal commitment to affordable housing declined, precipitously in the Reagan administration, putting a halt to serious efforts to develop new housing for low-income people."

The proposal to create a national housing trust fund financed by surpluses in federal mortgage insurance programs had 189 co-sponsors in the House and 27 in the Senate. It is backed by more than 3,000 organizations and individuals around the country, including housing and community advocacy groups, religious congregations, civil rights groups, labor unions, municipalities, elected officials, and others. The idea also may have popular support. A poll commissioned by the National Housing Trust Fund Campaign says that 62 percent believe there is a shortage of affordable rental housing in their communities, 66 percent believe Congress should act to solve the problem, and 66 percent back the idea of a trust fund once it is explained to them.

HUD opposes the idea of financing a trust fund through Federal Housing Administration insurance funds, drawing a distinction between reserves necessary to the health of the system and what advocates call surpluses. Tapping the reserves, a HUD spokesman says, could lead to insolvency in federal mortgage insurance accounts. "It's stealing from Peter to pay Paul," he says. HUD hasn't taken a stance on the broader idea of a national trust fund.

Representative Bernard Sanders, a Vermont independent, was expected to offer the trust fund proposal as an amendment to H.R.3995, an omnibus housing bill, when it came to the floor this fall. At press time, however, it was unclear if the house leadership would allow the bill to reach the floor, and advocates are digging in for the long haul, working to win further endorsements and encouraging local groups to lobby their legislators.

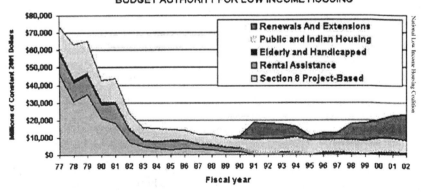

BUDGET AUTHORITY FOR LOW INCOME HOUSING

V. Revitalizing the
Urban Environment

Editor's Introduction

U rban planning is not only concerned with utilitarian issues such as transportation problems and housing shortages; it is also about looking ahead to the future, envisioning ways to improve our cities and our quality of life. What constitutes a "better" community is, of course, always a value judgment. The articles in this section present only a few of the many efforts being made in cities across the country to revitalize the urban environment.

For many, architecture is at the heart of urban planning. Nicolai Ouroussoff, in "At the Elite's Altar," argues that while American architecture has experienced a creative resurgence in recent years, that resurgence has been a relatively shallow one. "Half a century ago," he writes, "architects could believe, with some justification, that they were drafting the cities of tomorrow, and that the work they did would have significant social impact." In America, he claims, visionary public works—of the kind that graced former eras and are still found today in Europe—have been replaced by high-profile projects for wealthy clients and corporate interests, reducing architecture to isolated incidents of aesthetic showmanship. Ouroussoff compares the state of architecture in the U.S. with the scene in Europe and suggests it may be time for Americans to return to idealism in urban planning.

In "L.A. Rising," Cathleen McGuigan and David Jefferson describe the transformation of downtown Los Angeles into a hip neighborhood for young urbanites. Tax incentives and zoning changes have cleared the way for developers to rehabilitate abandoned industrial sites into trendy lofts for artists and professionals. To make the neighborhood more attractive to newcomers, architects are designing public plazas and ambitious cultural institutions, such as Frank Gehry's new Walt Disney Concert Hall for the Los Angeles Philharmonic, for which the County of Los Angeles provided the land and some of the funding.

In Portland, Oregon, city officials are spearheading a new approach to building design that benefits both the environment and city residents. In "Gardens Top It Off in Portland," Gillian Flaccus explains how the city is offering incentives to developers to build "ecoroofs"—roofs covered in foliage—as part of an attempt to better manage flooding after rainstorms. These living roofs, which are common in some European countries and are beginning to emerge in major American cities, not only reduce runoff but help counter pollution and can significantly reduce a building's energy costs.

In Atlanta, Georgia, construction is under way at Atlantic Station, Jacoby Development Corporation's massive $2 billion, 138-acre brownfield redevelopment project. Janet Frankston, in "At Atlantic Station Green(space) Is Huge,"

139

explains that the project was made possible through the Environmental Protection Agency (EPA) program known as Project XL, which allows companies to replace or simplify regulatory requirements if they agree to make changes that will achieve better environmental results than would have been obtained under existing regulations. Since Atlanta is currently out of compliance with federal transportation conformity requirements, it is not allowed to use federal funds to add to its highway system or construct certain types of transportation projects that require federal approval, even if they are not federally funded. Jacoby Development was able to secure funding and develop this transportation project by employing smart-growth strategies, such as including open spaces, pedestrian walkways, bike lanes, and a mass-transit system.

The role of the business community in shaping the future of Chicago, Illinois, is the subject of Alan Ehrenhalt's article "Urban Vision Through Corporate Ayes." Ehrenhalt writes, "Big things rarely get built in any city or metropolitan area without the active participation of the economic elite." Echoing a trend found in other areas of the country, Chicago's Commercial Club has emerged as the major sponsor of Metropolis 2020, a comprehensive regional plan that calls for area-wide land-use planning and stresses the availability of affordable housing and reliable mass transit. Ehrenhalt notes that although it may prove a challenge to gain the cooperation of suburban leadership, the plan calls for the creation of a Regional Coordinating Council to manage the effort.

One of the most watched urban planning projects currently under way is the redevelopment of the World Trade Center site in lower Manhattan, where, on September 11, 2001, the Twin Towers were destroyed in a terrorist attack. The rebuilding process has been highly contentious from the outset, as planners struggle to find a solution that will satisfy the public desire for a meaningful tribute, placate private interests by including adequate commercial and office space, and ensure that the end result fits into the larger vision of the city's present and future. The architect Daniel Libeskind was recently selected in a high-profile competition to lead the design, but disagreements remain among the various parties that have a stake in the project: the Port Authority of New York and New Jersey, which owns the site; developer Larry Silverstein, who holds the lease; Westfield America, which owned the mall beneath the towers; New York Governor George Pataki; Mayor Michael Bloomberg; and the Lower Manhattan Development Corporation. Casey Nelson Blake's article "Mourning and Modernism After 9/11"—written shortly after the initial round of designs, presented in July 2002, were thrown out due to public outcry denouncing their lack of imagination—focuses on the deeply felt desire for a public place of mourning and grief. Blake recounts the history of the Twin Towers and their relationship to the modernist movement and suggests that the modernist design of such public places as the Hiroshima Memorial Peace Park in Japan can serve as a guide for the future of New York City's ground zero.

At the Elite's Altar[1]

By Nicolai Ouroussoff
THE LOS ANGELES TIMES, DECEMBER 1, 2002

The past few years have been bountiful ones for American architecture. It is hard to name a major American city that doesn't have a significant civic project in the works, most by big-name talents. Art institutions, philharmonic boards and universities have turned to architects to raise their public profiles with flamboyant new buildings. The newly minted rich commission houses by cutting-edge talents as a way of achieving the cultural status they crave.

What is more, the stylistic range of these works makes this one of the most creative times in recent architectural history. Free of Modernism's once dogmatic formulas, architects continue to push the limits of aesthetic experimentation. The dynamic, futuristic forms of Zaha Hadid, the stoic mysticism of Tadao Ando, the aggressive conceptual constructions of Rem Koolhaas—such visions and others represent a remarkable range of competing values. Each is leaving its mark on the architectural landscape.

But if architecture's creative resurgence has once again caught the attention of the American public, that resurgence has also been relatively shallow. Half a century ago, architects could believe, with some justification, that they were drafting the cities of tomorrow, and that the work they did would have significant social impact.

Today, architects working in America are confined to serving a relatively small and entrenched elite—the corporate kingpins and aging philanthropists who typically make up the boards of the country's major cultural institutions. The success of the conservative political agenda has meant that the kind of visionary public works projects that remain possible in Europe are no longer part of the public dialogue here. The nation's faltering economy, meanwhile, has resulted in cuts in philanthropic spending.

The result is that architecture risks being reduced to a purely aesthetic game—one that offers the veneer of progress without its substance. At best, the high end of the profession is able to produce the occasional transcendent masterpiece. At worst, it functions as a mere plaything for the rich and their institutions.

"It is a time when everything seems possible but nothing is," says Koolhaas, architecture's reigning radical voice. "There is this cult of the masterpiece and the rest—a generic, unimaginative landscape. The middle ground is lost."

Culture and Commissions

The shift away from work that serves a broader public is not essentially the fault of architects. They do not set the country's political agenda, nor can they create commissions out of thin air—someone has to pay for them. But the explosion in high-profile cultural commissions has produced a sort of feeding frenzy among many architectural firms, which regularly vie against one another for the most prestigious—and lucrative—jobs. And that new focus has turned attention away from issues that once were at the heart of the profession.

The greatest monuments being built in America today are part of a cultural rather than political agenda. British high-tech Modernist Norman Foster, for example, is completing a major addition to Boston's Museum of Fine Arts; Daniel Libeskind, the designer of Berlin's celebrated Jewish Museum, is working on an addition to the Denver Art Museum; Koolhaas' Seattle Public Library is under construction; and Ando's Modern Art Museum of Fort Worth opens later this month.

The greatest monuments being built in America today are part of a cultural rather than political agenda.

Other projects are conspicuous emblems of American affluence. Richard Meier, the designer of the Getty Center, is completing two shimmering glass condominium towers overlooking Manhattan's Hudson River. Most of the apartments have been snatched up by such celebrities as Calvin Klein and Nicole Kidman. (Plagued by insider trading accusations, decorating doyen Martha Stewart is reportedly trying to unload her duplex for $8 million.)

Meier has also designed a stunning house in Malibu for billionaire Eli Broad. The house's pristine, sharp-edged white forms evoke the precision of a fine-tuned Swiss watch. In Napa Valley, the Swiss team of Jacques Herzog and Pierre de Meuron is completing a residence for the art collectors Richard and Pamela Kramlich. The project's undulating glass walls, set underneath a swooping faceted roof, evoke the intricacy of a Fabergé egg. Koolhaas' most recently completed design is a $40 million Prada boutique in Manhattan's SoHo district.

Such commissions have made these architects international celebrities. Their names are regularly sprinkled across the pages of glossy magazines; the unveiling of one of their buildings is often a major media event.

What that popularity has not given them, however, is access to the kind of large-scale public projects that could have a deeper social impact in this country. The American nuclear family, for example, has undergone a seismic shift in its identity in the postwar years—including the growth of single-parent households and gay marriages. These shifts raise profound questions about housing design, yet architects have barely begun to explore them. Big commercial and retail developments, meanwhile, are typically entrusted to mainstream, commercial architects who churn out the same formulaic atrocities.

No American city reflects this condition more pointedly than Los Angeles. The city has embarked on a number of major civic projects, from José Raphael Moneo's recently completed Cathedral of Our Lady of the Angels to Frank Gehry's Walt Disney Concert Hall, scheduled to open next fall, and Koolhaas' plan for a new Los Angeles County Museum of Art, currently in design stages. (Koolhaas' project is now on hold after voters defeated a bond measure to fund the building.)

These are all significant designs, and their addition to the city's civic landscape is invaluable. But the location of these projects is telling. The most visible cultural complex completed here over the last decade—the Getty Center—looms over one of the city's most exclusive neighborhoods, on a hilltop overlooking the 405 Freeway in Brentwood. Disney Hall and the cathedral are located downtown amid a mix of corporate towers and government offices that civic boosters are seeking to make palatable for tourists and middle-class suburbanites.

The notion of a similar civic undertaking being built in the Latino enclave of Boyle Heights or the predominantly African American neighborhoods of South-Central Los Angeles, by comparison, seems as likely as Steven Spielberg holding a premiere party in Watts.

Meanwhile, a bond issue that would have raised nearly $200 million for the expansion of two of the city's most important cultural institutions—the Los Angeles County Museum of Art and the Museum of Natural History—failed to pass in November. Another bond measure, which will provide $2.1 billion for the creation or renovation of up to 134,000 units of public housing in California, was approved. Yet state officials have no plans to explore how the new housing could fit into a larger conception of the region's growth, nor have they given any thought to how imaginative architecture could contribute to the lives of its inhabitants.

American architecture was not always so lacking in idealistic fervor. In the 1930s, when Frank Lloyd Wright first began promoting his Usonian houses, his intent was to offer a radical model for the American middle-class way of life. The houses' modest scale, horizontal profiles and free-flowing interiors evoked an Emersonian vision of man in harmony with the natural world. About the same time, inspired by the grand urban schemes then being proposed by the European avant-garde, Wright designed Broadacre City, a theoretical suburban arcadia of single-family homes and sweeping landscapes punctuated by the occasional skyscraper.

In Los Angeles, faith in architecture's transformative powers survived through the early 1960s, when mainstream developers were churning out suburban middle-class housing tracts whose streamlined appearance, two-car garages and humming appliances were held up as an emblem of America's unwavering faith in its own future.

That faith collapsed in the 1970s, when it became apparent that Modernism could not solve society's ills; at its worst, it contributed to them.

"The Modernist Utopia was only achieved in a negative way," Libeskind says. "In the name of helping people, they only created dull, conformist environments. And that was the end of ideology in architecture."

But broader political forces were also at play. By the 1980s, the social activism of New Deal-era America was beginning to fade, picked apart by the advances of free-market capitalism and corporate globalism.

In architecture schools today, it is still possible to find programs like Auburn University's Rural Studio, which designs and builds low-cost homes for Alabama's poor. But such programs are limited in ambition, and students now are far more likely to be engaged by issues like "corporate branding," as if the profession's function were no different from that of a national advertising firm—to create slick,

---

"In the name of helping people, [Modernists] only created dull, conformist environments. And that was the end of ideology in architecture."—Daniel Libeskind, architect

---

captivating images for high-profile clients.

"I think that the most important change has been the rising adulation of the market," Koolhaas said, "and the disappearance of the state. It has reduced everything [in America] to this question of profit and consumption."

That assessment only gets bleaker when compared with what architects have been able to accomplish in Europe over the past decades. While Americans were loudly proclaiming the death of the Utopian dream, Europe went on tinkering with the old models, fine-tuning them, lowering—but not abandoning—expectations.

In the 1960s, for example, groups like the London-based Archigram and the Italian collaborative Superstudio were producing a stream of theoretical projects that sought to transform Modernism's increasingly limiting formulas into a less oppressive vision of the future. Superstudio's 1969 "Continuous Monument," for example, proposed gargantuan rationalist glass-and-steel structures that would have extended endlessly across a medieval European landscape and were meant to function as refuges from commercial culture.

Such projects were essentially theoretical fantasies, but their impact was felt nonetheless. With its scaffolding-like exterior of steel pipes and transparent tubes, Paris' Pompidou Center, for example, was a direct descendant of Archigram's Fun City proposal. Both were conceived as flexible frameworks for a more spontaneous culture.

A decade later, French President François Mitterrand launched one of the most ambitious building programs in recent Parisian history, creating half a dozen major civic monuments, most of them in the city's working-class eastern sector. The idea was to rectify the imbalance between the city's traditional core, packed with historic monuments, and an area of the city that had none.

In preparation for the 1992 Olympics in Barcelona, the Spanish government devised a plan that created a vast range of new public spaces, significantly enriching the city's civic identity. The scope of the development also spawned a major revival in contemporary Spanish and Portuguese architecture, uncovering a range of new talents like Alvaro Siza, Carme Pinós and Enric Miralles.

And in the Netherlands, a more egalitarian country than the U.S., government planners have created hundreds of thousands of new units of social housing in the past decade, asking many of the country's emerging architectural talents to come up with a humane vision for their design.

Clumped in a Core

It is not hard to imagine the impact such strategies could have had on a city like Los Angeles. Rather than concentrating the majority of our civic and cultural institutions in a single civic core, they could have been dispersed across the city—a Latino museum in East L.A. or a LACMA branch in South-Central. (Vague promises of extensive new development in South-Central, in fact, were made after the 1992 Los Angeles riots, but they were never kept.)

Similarly, L.A.'s Catholic archdiocese might have considered building a network of parish churches in the city's most blighted areas rather than concentrating all of its resources on the Cathedral of Our Lady of the Angels. The cathedral is a monument to the church's power; the smaller churches might have signaled a more egalitarian spiritual vision. (In Rome, Richard Meier is completing just such a project, a stunning church whose gleaming white forms act as a spiritual beacon in an otherwise bleak landscape of decrepit housing blocks.)

Such an approach could have given these communities a deeper sense of cultural identity. It could make invisible communities suddenly visible, weaving them into the city's broader cultural fabric. But the idea was never discussed.

Like other architects who have struggled with how to recapture architecture's social relevance, Libeskind claims the answer is not to abandon hope, but to return to a more humanist vision of architecture's role.

"A life without utopian dreams would not be worth living," he says. "But I think the ethics now evolves from dealing directly with the human condition. Architecture should be thought of more like surgery than mathematics."

Pipe dreams? Maybe. But architecture and city planning in this country could use an infusion of idealism. We are the richest country in the world. Our architects rank among the most creative. Why not invest some of that creativity where it is needed most?

L.A. Rising[2]

By Cathleen McGuigan and David Jefferson
Newsweek, November 11, 2002

If you stand on the rooftop terrace of the chic new Standard hotel in downtown Los Angeles, you might think you're in a real city. From the top of the 12-story high-rise conversion—built in 1956 as the headquarters of Superior Oil—you look out at a glittering forest of glass-and-steel towers. The scene on the roof is jammed and noisy, as cool twentysomethings jostle for elbow room at the bar or colonize the red podlike cabanas by the pool. But it's not real—it's more like a movie. If you go down to the swanky Standard lobby, with its marble floors and hot pink sofas, and walk outside, the bubble bursts. The streets don't bustle like Chicago's or New York's—they're dark and empty. The Standard's stylish urbanity is a goof on the visions of long-dead tycoons, who once powwowed next door at the elite California Club and who built this part of town—which, with its formal brand of sleek corporate modernism, is irrelevant to the culture of pink stucco and palm trees that we think of when we think of Los Angeles.

But despite the fact that the sidewalks roll up at sunset, downtown L.A. has gotten hot. We know this sounds familiar—the neighborhood's had more comebacks than Richard Gere. Now developers, spurred by tax incentives, are busy flipping dilapidated buildings into lofts, and young urban pioneers are moving in, lured by the affordable rents and the vague notion that urban living is cool. The first downtown movie studio has opened, at the old Unocal headquarters, where the prequel to *Terminator* is now shooting. The once fringy art scene—with struggling artists tucked into abandoned industrial spaces—is flourishing, and new galleries are turning up in Chinatown. The most avant-garde of L.A.'s design schools, SCI-Arc, moved downtown last year from the west side. And everyone's talking about the hugely ambitious architecture projects going up. "The most innovative architects in southern California in the 20th century were really involved in the private sector, doing domestic homes," says Richard Koshalek, director emeritus of the Museum of Contemporary Art (MoCA). "Now these talents are focused on the public realm."

It's not just that world-class architects like L.A.'s own Frank Gehry are building big here—it's that they're accommodating street life and pedestrians in a way this car-crazy city hasn't done before. No project is more anticipated than Gehry's Walt Disney Concert Hall for the L.A. Philharmonic, on Grand Avenue next to the old Dorothy Chandler Pavilion. Almost 15 years in the plan-

---

ning, its gorgeous stainless-steel sail-like shapes are now unfurling at the crest of Bunker Hill. Even though the opening's a year away, the buzz has begun among design buffs and music lovers of all stripes (Jennifer Lopez just used it as a location for her new video "Jenny From the Block"). Down the street is MoCA, while a little farther north is the just-opened, controversial new cathedral, Our Lady of the Angels, designed by the eminent Spanish architect Rafael Moneo. The city fathers are putting a lot of faith in this cultural corridor—though a design scheme by Gehry, Moneo and MoCA architect Arata Isozaki, to make the avenue more pedestrian-friendly, never got off the ground. Still, Gehry's making the concert hall alluring to the ordinary passerby. "On the corner I made an outdoor foyer, a public space where people could sit, maybe brown-bag it at lunch," he says. Moneo's amber concrete cathedral is less inviting: the church doors don't even face the street but rather a private plaza in back, surrounded by fortress-like walls, with gates that shut at night. But throngs of people come during the day, including office workers at lunchtime who perch at the outdoor cafe. Meanwhile, a few blocks to the east, the ground's been broken for the Caltrans center. A transportation agency doesn't sound glamorous, but the design by L.A. architect Thom Mayne's firm Morphosis will bring an edgy 21st-century scheme to the 'hood. Mayne's also planned a vast public plaza to encourage the kind of hanging out that pumps life into a city.

> *"Downtowns aren't built with Disney halls and cathedrals."*—Tom Gilmore, developer

But the main way to keep the urban energy up is to get people to live there. "Downtowns aren't built with Disney halls and cathedrals," says developer Tom Gilmore, who's been converting decaying historic buildings into loft apartments since the late '90s. He's attracted plenty of tenants, despite an urban grittiness right out of the movies: no one in his 237-unit Old Bank District lofts seems to mind the bird's-eye view of Skid Row's Midnight Mission. His latest project is the conversion of the 1913 Gothic Revival El Dorado Hotel, most recently a flophouse. He's also involved in transforming the earthquake-shaken old cathedral, St. Vibiana's, into an arts center and apartments. Today, there're more than 5,000 downtown market-rate rentals, from $1,000 to $4,000 a month—with another 5,000 planned for the next three years, plus 8,500 affordable units. Still, that's not a lot of residents, considering the daytime population of downtown swells to 300,000. When it comes right down to it, the future of downtown L.A. may hinge on a fancy supermarket: the nearest one is a seven-mile commute. But the first name-brand supermarket is still two years off, part of a $200 million mixed-use project by the CIM development group. Dry cleaners, laundries and other amenities are hard to come by, too. And can you live without a car? Mmmm, maybe. There are plans to extend the subway, which is essential to creating more street life.

Part of the area's appeal is its diversity—Chinatown, Little Tokyo, the Latino shops along Broadway. "In many ways, L.A. is a segregated city," says architect Eric Owen Moss, director of SCI-Arc. "But downtown those pieces bump together." Still, it's a fragile ecology, with many low-income residents—including artists who moved downtown years ago—being pushed out by rising rents. And stricter enforcement of anti-loitering laws is hurting the homeless. "They tell us no more sleeping in cardboard boxes, so we have to get moving by 4 A.M.," says Terry Johnson, who's lived on and off downtown streets for years. He maintains that without people like him, downtown will become "another Burbank."

Burbank? We don't think so. That ineffable "cool" factor seems to be sticking. Just look at the art and design scene. SCI-Arc is ensconced in its new downtown home east of Little Tokyo—in a former railroad-freight terminal that's a quarter-mile long (some of the 470 students get from their studio desks to class on skateboards or scooters). Nearby is the Gehry-designed Geffen Contemporary Museum, and next door is the site of a future children's museum designed by Thom Mayne. In Chinatown, along with artists' studios and new galleries, a former restaurant is getting a makeover into a bar to cater to the art scene. (Who needs supermarkets—these downtown denizens need clubs!) "There's been a steady stream of cool young people coming through," says the Standard hotel's owner, Andre Balazs. "You always had a kind of corporate infrastructure there, but until a young urban settler adopts the neighborhood, no urban center can go anywhere." Consider the neighborhood adopted. Other observers agree that downtown L.A.'s moment has arrived at last. Fernando Torres-Gil, vice president of the city-planning commission under Mayor Tom Bradley, bought a condo opposite the new Gehry concert hall three years ago (it's since doubled in value). "After decades of failed attempts," he says, "we're finally seeing the emergence of a 24-hour community right here in downtown." And not just on the rooftop of the Standard.

Gardens Top It Off in Portland[3]

By Gillian Flaccus
The Los Angeles Times, December 15, 2002

When Chris Moehling wants to show off the new garden at the youth hostel he manages, he steps out a second-story bedroom window onto a roof blooming with plants.

The 650-square-foot garden of scrubby succulents and yellow marigolds grows right out of the roof, above the busy street, and is visible to the hundreds of shoppers and motorists who pass below.

"We get people walking in from the street asking all kinds of questions," Moehling said. "This is one of the more visible streets in town. People really get a kick out of it."

The hostel's plantings are the latest in a string of green spaces flourishing on Portland's roofs in place of traditional shingles and tar—and the trend is no coincidence.

The city has emerged as an international leader in the budding "ecoroof" movement. Portland has boosted its reputation by enacting regulations that offer breaks to developers who install green roofs and by officials who aggressively promote rooftop planting.

Living roofs, long common in Germany, Holland and Switzerland, can reduce runoff after rainstorms by as much as 90%, slash a building's energy costs by 10%, and reduce summer temperatures on scorching city rooftops by about 70 degrees, experts say.

They also delay the runoff after a major storm by several hours, preventing flooding and sewage problems that occur when a storm-water system overflows.

And the gardens filter pollutants and heavy metals from rainwater and cool the excess water before it enters streams and threatens sensitive aquatic species, such as salmon in the Pacific Northwest.

"Once a person sees all the things that an ecoroof can do, it's almost dumb not to plant them," said Tom Liptan, an environmental specialist for the city. "I expect we'll see a lot more."

Portland isn't the only city to plant gardens on its skyline.

Chicago, Toronto and Seattle have grown gardens on their city halls and courthouses, and Atlanta plans to follow suit. Ford Motor Co. will finish a 10.6-acre living roof on its truck plant in Dearborn, Mich., next year, and county buildings in Anne Arundel County, Md., have recently sprouted grassy tops.

What sets Portland apart, experts say, is the city's financial commitment to ecoroofs in the form of tax breaks, grants and building codes, and the range of buildings—both public and private—that sport rooftop gardens.

---

3. Reprinted with permission of The Associated Press.

"If you look at it on the surface, offering economic incentives makes a lot of sense," said David Beattie, director of the Center for Green Roof Research at Pennsylvania State University.

"We have to drag people to the table, so having economic incentives such as you have in Portland is the way to do it."

Portland took the lead in the tiny, but growing, green roof movement nearly two years ago when it approved a regulation that allows developers to expand their building plans if they include an ecoroof. Experts say Portland is the only city in North America to offer such an incentive; it also waives certain code requirements for those with green roofs.

In the future, Portland may create zoning that encourages ecoroofs or offer significant discounts on storm-water fees for people who cultivate their rooftops, said Dean Marriott, Portland's director of environmental services.

"I've just been talking this up to anyone who will listen," he said. "We're trying to get public and private examples of ecoroofs in the community, and we're trying to use all the incentives that we can think of."

Portland took the lead in the tiny, but growing, green roof movement nearly two years ago.

Portland hopes that green roofs will help end the severe and recurring sewage overflows that pour into the Columbia and Willamette rivers after nearly every heavy rainstorm by reducing the amount of water runoff. The runoff floods the system, forcing raw sewage into nearby rivers.

Under federal mandate, the city must correct the problem by 2011. It's in the middle of a $1 billion project to install larger underground pipes, said Liptan, city environmental specialist.

Portland has made government incentives for green roofs a priority because of the technology's cost. Green roofs cost about two times more than regular roofs to install—between $10 and $15 per square foot—and require extensive research and planning.

Financial support from the government is key to persuading companies and individuals to install ecoroofs, said Ireen Wieditz, director of the Toronto-based Green Roofs for Healthy Cities.

"There's always a lot of interest, but I think it's still new to a lot of people," she said. "People seem to love the idea and are really embracing it, but we just need the government to support it."

Faced with crowding, runoff and pollution problems, some German cities require new flat roofs to be green roofs, while others require residents to pay taxes based on the percentage of paved surface they own.

As a result, one out of seven German roofs are green; in some cities, one-fourth of buildings have ecoroofs, said Beattie, the Penn State professor.

"Man has an amazing capacity to dirty his own nest and the Germans have done it before we did," he said. "They simply faced the problem before we did."

Liptan is encouraged by recent interest in ecoroofs, however, and said he has fielded nearly two dozen serious phone calls in recent weeks.

At least five major city developments are considering ecoroofs, and a new nonprofit called "Ecoroofs Everywhere" is working with the city to spur interest in the technology among homeowners and small businesses.

To Greg Haines, the man who started Ecoroofs Everywhere, that's fitting news.

"I think of Portland as the No. 1 ecoroof city because storm water is such a big deal here and salmon are so huge and the Willamette River runs right through the city," he said. "When I think of Portland, I think of the bridges and the river and the community."

At Atlantic Station, Green(space) Is Huge[4]

By Janet Frankston
The Atlanta Journal-Constitution, April 21, 2003

After looking at a panoramic view of the development from the conference room window of Atlantic Station's Midtown offices [in Atlanta, Ga.], we drove to the site across the Downtown Connector and walked around.

Jim Jacoby's Atlantic Station, the mini-city now under construction in Midtown, has been called many things: massive, expensive, important.

Yet Jacoby wants one more description: green, as in a national environmental model.

With the help of the federal Environmental Protection Agency, the state and the city of Atlanta—and with financial backing from one of the country's largest insurance companies—it could earn that distinction.

"There's gold in environmental redevelopment," says Jacoby, 59, chairman and chief executive officer of Jacoby Development. His company is developing the $2 billion project with partner American International Group.

He recently walked around the emerging Atlantic Station to talk about the environmental benefits of "smart growth," which seeks to mix uses, preserve open land, create communities where people can walk and provide transportation choices.

Before Atlantic Station, Jacoby developed strip centers with Wal-Marts. Now, he's the owner of the Marineland park in Florida and regularly convenes an "eco lunch bunch" with like-minded developers and conservationists. A recent guest was Parris Glendening, the former governor of Maryland who created a statewide smart-growth program.

But don't call Jacoby an environmentalist.

"I'm a developer first," he says. "Hopefully we can have a little bit of influence on the way we develop."

If other developers see Atlantic Station as profitable, perhaps they will try some of Jacoby's techniques, he says. He points to the project's stormwater retention pond. The land is being reused as an elliptical-shaped 2-acre lake.

---

4. *The Atlanta Journal-Constitution*, "At Atlantic Station, Green (space) Is Huge" by Janet Frankston. Copyright © 2003 by *The Atlanta Journal-Constitution*. Reproduced with permission of *The Atlanta Journal-Constitution* in the format Other Book via Copyright Clearance Center.

"It's an amenity, and it's also functional," says Jacoby, wearing a tie with a dolphin pattern. "This is how you maximize the use of very important land."

A steel footbridge spans the shallow lake, surrounded by 4 acres of parkland. It sits on expensive real estate, but the area will become a public space where residents, neighbors, and shoppers can gather, he says, with a backdrop of the Midtown skyline behind him.

The 138-acre project is located west of the Downtown Connector, on the once-polluted Atlantic Steel mill site. About 165,000 tons of contaminated soil were hauled away during site cleanup.

When it's completed over the next decade, Atlantic Station expects to have 6 million square feet of Class A office space; 3,000 to 5,000 apartments, houses, and townhomes; 1.5 million square feet of retail space, including restaurants and movie theaters; and 1,000 hotel rooms.

Jacoby said he spent $2 million to $3 million on environmental studies before he purchased the land in 1997. Initial construction costs came in at $250 million, including a 25-acre parking deck.

Jacoby would like to see people use Atlantic Station's sidewalks and trails for exercising. They'll be able to walk within the development and across the 17th Street bridge.

"If people are healthier, AIG is going to get a better return on [its] investment as an insurance company," he says, with all seriousness.

Of the bridge's nine lanes, five will be restricted to pedestrians, bicycle riders and a shuttle bus. Atlantic Station will pay for the shuttles and the $2 million annual operating expenses for them to circle between the development and the Arts Center MARTA station every four minutes.

Yellow steel beams forming the base of the $38 million bridge have stretched across the Connector for nearly two months. Jacoby watches the progress from his conference room window in a Midtown high-rise. The bridge should be finished by the end of the year.

Atlantic Station is part of EPA's Project XL, which supports ways to achieve cost-effective public health and environmental protection. The status helped secure funding for the bridge when Atlanta's federal road money stopped flowing because of dirty air.

Jacoby says Atlantic Station will show other environmental benefits beyond improving air quality by keeping some cars off roads.

The stormwater and sanitary sewage systems will be kept apart. The separation will prevent stormwater from overwhelming the sewer treatment system, making the treatment of sanitary waste more efficient.

In addition, the retail and office space will use a central chilling system instead of individual air conditioning units. While upfront costs to tenants may be more, their energy bills are expected to be lower, he says.

"Not only is it better for the environment and future cost savings, but it'll be an aesthetic," he says. The rooftops will not have cooling units atop them.

Another aesthetic: Atlantic Station has planted 2,800 trees within the site and surrounding neighborhood.

"I signed a check for a bunch of them," he gripes, but adds, "It's all about the quality of life, bringing trees and oxygen."

Urban Vision Through Corporate Ayes[5]

By Alan Ehrenhalt
Governing, June 2002

Once upon a time in this country, architects did everything they could to sound like romantic poets. Generations of history students have faithfully copied down Daniel Burnham's pompous but powerful admonition to "make no little plans—they have no magic to stir men's blood."

For sheer metaphorical grandiosity, however, I like a different Burnhamism, one he included in his Chicago revitalization program of 1909. "The great flowers of fine arts," Burnham wrote, "are born on the stalk of commercial supremacy."

On this occasion, the famous architect was being not only florid but also politically prudent. His master plan had been underwritten by Chicago's Commercial Club, the organization of local manufacturing and mercantile interests. In order to obtain future support for his artistic visions of a City Beautiful, it made sense to play to the vanity of the interests that could afford to underwrite it.

On the other hand, it's hard to quarrel with the main point. Dreams of metropolitan greatness, particularly dreams that involve the construction of large projects such as office towers, parks and bridges, nearly always require enthusiasm from the prevailing corporate elite—the equivalent of the meatpackers, department store owners and railroad tycoons of Burnham's time. "It has been so," the architect proclaimed, "from Athens to Chicago."

It certainly was so in the Chicago of the early 20th century. During the two decades that followed publication of Burnham's plan, much of his vision was realized. Not all of it—Burnham's idea of a monumental new civic center remained on the shelf—but the majority of the 1909 plan came to pass: huge parks, forest preserves, a pristine downtown lakefront and a wide, promenade-like boulevard connecting the north and south banks of the Chicago River. There are many reasons why Chicago escaped much of the center-city blight that afflicted most of urban America in recent years, but the 1909 plan is at least part of the explanation.

If it worked a century ago, could it work again? An experiment is underway to find out, promoted by none other than the Commercial Club, which is flexing its aging muscles as the prime sponsor of a new regional master plan, Metropolis 2020, and of a permanent organization of the same name, dedicated to bringing the plan into effect.

History does not repeat itself, of course. Many of the elements of local politics in Chicago, as in any city, have changed beyond recognition in 90 years. The Commercial Club itself is no longer the preserve of merchants, manufacturers and meatpackers—as many of its activists now seem to come from academia, philanthropy and social service as from corporate boardrooms.

But Burnham's fundamental insight remains valid: Big things rarely get built in any city or metropolitan area without the active participation of the economic elite. If Metropolis 2020 represents the thinking of the current elite—the banks, the law firms, the real estate investors and the remnant of manufacturing influence (and it clearly does represent them)—it is worth studying carefully as a clue to important future events.

Considered that way, Metropolis 2020 is a remarkable document. It commits Chicago's civic leadership to a New Urbanist platform of public transit, pedestrian-oriented neighborhoods, mixed-income zoning, area-wide land use planning, substantial environmental remediation and a brand-new Regional Coordinating Council with bonding authority to bring the whole package together.

Big things rarely get built in any city or metropolitan area without the active participation of the economic elite.

One might be tempted to view the Metropolis 2020 program as an odd departure from traditional corporate orthodoxy, except that it isn't really unusual anymore. Something fairly similar is going on in quite a few cities around the country. In the words of George Ranney, the president of Metropolis 2020, "there's a sense of restlessness and concern in the business community right now." The restlessness extends far beyond Chicago.

Atlanta may be the best example. Two years ago, when the Georgia legislature voted to create a Regional Transportation Authority, with broad land use planning powers, it was the Atlanta Chamber of Commerce that did most of the work. The Chamber managed the entire process, from drafting to lobbying to media relations. Since its creation, the regional authority has taken small, cautious steps toward freeing metropolitan Atlanta from its 20th-century dependence on the automobile. But the business community has taken larger steps, including the relocation of major facilities from the suburbs to the central city in an effort to reduce commuting time, congestion and ozone emissions.

You see it in California's Silicon Valley, where the CEOs and middle managers of the major technology companies are finding the pleasures of corporate success compromised by highway congestion that makes it difficult for them to leave their offices and go anywhere during large portions of the day. These are people who don't need to be sold on Smart Growth; more often than not these days, they are the ones trying to sell it to others.

It is this same link between mobility and economics that drives much of the Metropolis 2020 report. Last year, in setting out a new set of "metropolis principles," the group argued bluntly that "the distance between housing, transportation and jobs can have a major impact on an employer's bottom line." Last August, more than 100 Chicago-area businesses, ranging from Allstate Insurance to United Airlines, signed a pledge to make future site-location decisions based in large part on whether a community offers housing "affordable to working people" and whether it "is served by reliable and accessible mass transit."

These same businesses are following a similar line on environmental issues. Last year, when Chicago staged a considerable coup by luring the corporate offices of Boeing Aircraft away from Seattle, one of the little-noticed parts of the deal was a $2 million commitment by the city to retrofit the corporate headquarters for energy efficiency. "Major companies want green and clean," Chicago's environment commissioner explained.

It may seem a long leap from the rather narrow issue of employee mobility to the Burnham-like sweep of a broad agenda that ranges from transit subsidies to green buildings. In fact, though, it makes political sense. As powerful as Chicago's corporate establishment may be, it requires allies. The breadth of the agenda helps create them. With virtually all the environmental groups and most labor unions inside the tent along with the corporate leadership, there aren't too many important interests left on the outside to protest.

So far, the only organized counterattack against Metropolis 2020 has come from the free-market Right. Early this year, the Chicago-based Heartland Institute issued a report taking the Commercial Club to task for what it called an "unjustified bias against auto travel and in favor of fixed-rail public transit use." But the report didn't make much of a splash. Grounded more in ideology than in practicality, it analyzed the mobility issue by proclaiming that "metropolitan residents simply travel too much." The institute recommended a drastically higher fuel tax, with corresponding reductions in the federal income tax, which it said "would induce enough movement of residences and elimination of frivolous driving to reduce car travel by 15 or 20 percent."

Possibly it would. But attacking congestion by telling people to stay home isn't a very appealing political program. In fact, the sheer implausibility of such proposals underscores the irrelevance of the whole critique. The only sensible conclusion one can draw from looking at the opposition to Metropolis 2020 is that there hasn't been any meaningful opposition at all.

That's not to say there won't be any. Most of the important things the Commercial Club wants to do require the approval of the Illinois legislature, where the Senate has been dominated for nearly a decade by suburban Republicans wary of regional solutions or any solutions at all that might appear to benefit the big urban octopus that Democrats control. "Suburbanites have been paying for Chicago forever," Senate president James "Pate" Philip warned a couple of years ago. "The free ride is over."

The legislature will be much easier to convince on Metropolis 2020 if it hears from the leadership of suburbs themselves, and particularly if suburban mayors argue that the idea of expanded public transit is popular with their constituents. Metropolis 2020 has been sensitive to this—it has two suburban mayors on its executive council and a popular former mayor on its staff. Suburban officials played a key role in the group's first real lobbying venture—a successful effort in 1999 to promote passage of Governor George Ryan's Illinois FIRST highway and infrastructure program.

But that was no more than a dry run. The really big things Metropolis 2020 wants to do—creating the Regional Coordinating Council, investing $500 million a year in transportation projects, subsidizing moderate-priced suburban housing to locate workers near their jobs—will be much more difficult to accomplish, especially at a time of state budget austerity.

Some of the important decisions on Metropolis 2020 are likely to be made by state government next year, and whatever happens at the polls this November, it will be a state government substantially different from the current one. A new governor, a new set of House and Senate districts, and heavy turnover in both chambers will give the proponents of the plan an unusual opportunity for salesmanship—but will likely create new and unforeseen obstacles along the way.

In the long run, though, what matters more than the fate of any of the individual proposals is the coalition that has taken shape around them and will take shape in other parts of metropolitan America over the next few years. As Daniel Burnham understood, it's never easy to sell an urban vision, especially when it costs a lot of money. But it's easier when there's a healthy roster of CEOs backing it up. And it's easier still when they are CEOs who have spent a few too many hours stuck in traffic.

Mourning and Modernism
After 9/11[6]

BY CASEY NELSON BLAKE
THE NATION, SEPTEMBER 23, 2002

The near-unanimous revulsion that the six original proposals for the former World Trade Center site provoked among New Yorkers was one of the most hopeful developments since the initial wave of solidarity washed through the city after the September 11 attacks. Once the proposals became public, it was evident that planners had badly misjudged the city's needs and desires. People searching for commemoration, healing and civic inspiration found instead interchangeable plans for an office mall in lower Manhattan. Real estate pressures trumped all other considerations, except for the political need to appease survivors and family members who demanded that the Twin Towers' "footprints" remain untouched "sacred ground." I know I was not the only critic of the original WTC who shook my head in frustration at the mediocrity on display and decided it would be far better to rebuild the original towers instead. A friend confessed his fantasy of a single, 200-story skyscraper—a giant finger pointed at the killers. At least that would speak to something honest in the city's soul.

The reluctant admission that we New Yorkers miss the towers, that we came to love them in spite of themselves, has become a cliché in post–9/11 journalism. Their destruction coincided with a moment when Modernism—after years of derision in academic and architectural circles—seemed again all the rage, though in this case an appreciation for clean, Modernist design was neatly severed from the social progressivism that inspired many of its adherents almost a century ago. In the fall of 2001, Modernism was again on the scene as a "style," not as a "movement," and the coffee-table books and magazines lavishly illustrated with images of Modernist icons carried only the slightest reference to the confident hope that many architects and planners had once held for satisfying popular demands for adequate housing and sanitary living conditions. In fact, by the time both towers were completed in 1973, the entire Modernist program for social reconstruction and urban renewal was in intellectual and political crisis, thanks to the work of critics such as Jane Jacobs, Lewis Mumford, Robert Venturi and William H. Whyte, and to the activism of those citizens who blocked bulldozers and made preservation and context the watchwords of a new historicist approach to urbanism. Whatever nostalgia may now exist for

6. "Mourning and Modernism after 9/11" by Casey Nelson Blake. Reprinted with permission from the September 23, 2002, issue of *The Nation*.

the Trade Center seems to be a longing for a bold New York sky-line, shaped more by daring than by death, and not for Modernism in its fuller, more expansive vision.

The World Trade Center had an ambiguous place in the history of Modernism, in any case. Ada Louise Huxtable noted as early as 1962 that architect Minoru Yamasaki's design displayed an "ornamental style and a conscious historicism" at odds with the spare function-alism of reigning Modernist orthodoxy. In a perceptive essay in last November's College Art Association newsletter, *CAA News*, Ned Kaufman quoted Huxtable's comments in an analysis that juxtaposed the failure of the WTC's vast Modernist plaza with the "vaguely Venetian arcades on which the towers stood." "What did the towers stand for, anyway?" Kaufman asked, if they were not examples of an unalloyed Modernist architectural vision. His answer was that they stood for the bureaucratic state. "The WTC was not an expression of free enterprise," he wrote: "It was built by Big Government, was roundly criticized for that, and in market terms could not have been called a good investment. . . . In symbol and substance, it was government projecting a design."

> *The Twin Towers arose out of the wreckage of urban liberalism like tombstones for Big Government.*

In this context, the ambivalence that so many New Yorkers had about the towers before September 11 may have reflected a much deeper uncertainty about Big Government and, more precisely, about the arrogant, top-down urban liberalism associated with Robert Moses and other master builders in the middle years of the past century. That liberalism was in retreat by the early 1970s, repudiated as much by liberals as by neoconservatives and others appalled at the fiscal crisis, crime and physical decay that followed on the upheavals of the 1960s. The Twin Towers arose out of the wreckage of urban liberalism like tombstones for Big Government, evoking memories of the promise of visionary planning on a grand scale and the utter failure of that vision in practice. No wonder they proved such an embarrassment. They were like the 1970s remake of *King Kong* filmed at the towers: an utterly graceless coda to the dazzling Modernist culture that had once given us the Chrysler and Empire State buildings, Fay Wray and Fiorello La Guardia.

For an intellectual left sliding into the dark pessimism of the mid- and late-1970s under the influence of the Frankfurt School and other sources, the WTC towers were the perfect embodiment of a Promethean will to mastery that trapped human life in Max Weber's "iron cage" of bureaucracy and technical control. Modern architecture, in this view, was the accomplice of a capitalist mod-ernization that had gutted cities of their historical centers and popular folkways in the name of progress. Long before the completion of the towers, Lewis Mumford had described the skyscraper as "a human filing cabinet" and decried the destruction of urban sociability by the highway, the downtown skyscraper and the suburb. Was not the erection of these gargantuan buildings that dwarfed the landscape and deprived office workers of easy access to air and light a sign that the Enlightenment project had ended in an inhuman cult of power? Mumford had by the 1960s already come to view the modern industrial city as an immense "necropolis." One imagines that he would have seen the strikes on the towers, and the horrific losses they produced, as somehow in keeping with an urbanism that sacrificed human needs to gigantic totems of technological and bureaucratic power. The Twin Towers, in this grim logic, were symbolic tombs for urban life long before Al Qaeda's murderers boarded their flights that terrible morning.

Whatever its implication in such narratives of progressive doom, the history of modern architecture and urban planning is more and other than a history of a failed liberal project, more and other than the nightmare of an Enlightenment rationality turned Frankenstein monster. Such accounts neglect the deep concern within the Modern movement for the demands of billions for civic dignity and a decent standard of living. The rebuilding of lower Manhattan provides an opportunity to move beyond a complacent confession of progressive failure and take stock of the resources still available to us from both the Modern movement and the social democratic reformism that was its lifeblood. As Kaufman shrewdly noted, "In its destruction the WTC put government back at the center of our consciousness: it is to government that injured people and businesses have reflexively turned for help—each level of government looking expectantly to the next—and it is government at the highest level that is now redesigning lives and deaths through decisions that affect us at every level—military deployments, homeland security, and much more." If the market fundamentalism of the past quarter-century is slowly giving way to an inchoate social liberalism, then perhaps it is also time to revisit the history of the Modern movement in architecture and planning as something more than an effort at social control or an episode in chic design.

One way to reapproach that history is to examine the way in which Modernism—as a truly "International Style"—has successfully created sites for grief and mourning. Modernism has at its best served those working through the traumatic history of the past century by combining a utopian sense of possibility with a heightened awareness of human limitation and loss. Americans would do well, as they contemplate their own tragedy, to consider the example of the Hiroshima Memorial Peace Park erected at the site of the first dropping of the atomic bomb by the United States on August 6, 1945. That Ground Zero—the first Ground Zero—has been much on my mind in recent months, as I have considered how New Yorkers and others have engaged in public practices of mourning those killed on September 11.

The Hiroshima Memorial Peace Park is a classic example of postwar architectural Modernism of the sort that passed out of fashion in the 1970s and '80s. The stark geometry of its plan, the austere and uninviting design of its museum buildings and the vast emptiness of its central spaces remind us of other Modernist plazas that now seem relics of some previous civilization. Whether we are looking at the memorial park in Hiroshima, the center of Brasília, the windswept center of Nelson Rockefeller's Albany, New York, or photographs of the original WTC plaza, we are in the presence of an International Style vision of orderly, utopian planning that now strikes many as sterile and lifeless.

The Peace Park in Hiroshima certainly opens itself up to such criticisms, as well as to the charge that mid-twentieth-century architectural Modernism imposed a blanket universalism on landscapes at the expense of difference and the particularities of local culture. The revisions of the Hiroshima landscape in the years since its design in the 1950s bear some resemblance to reactions in

---

Modernism provided people around the world with an urban language and public places for mourning in the years after [World War II].

---

the United States and Europe against the universalist claims of urban Modernism. Protests against the exclusion of any reference to the tens of thousands of forced Korean laborers who died in Hiroshima led first to the erection in 1970 of a Korean memorial outside the perimeter of the park and then to the movement of that memorial inside the park itself in 1999. Likewise, the Peace Memorial Museum has had to revise the story it tells about the war and the events of August 6 in ways that promote a more critical, multiperspectival reading of Japan's actions in World War II. Such revisions resemble the public rescripting of U.S. history in recent years to include the stories of excluded groups, and they have provoked controversies familiar to those who have watched the battles over recent exhibitions at the Smithsonian.

What surprised me, when I visited the Peace Park in June 1999, was the way it revealed how Modernism provided people around the world with an urban language and public places for mourning in the years after the war. Perhaps the plain, geometrical design of the Peace Park appealed to visitors as an appropriate response to trauma, and not simply as an image of a streamlined urban modernity for a war-ravaged world. By creating clean, open spaces for reflection and self-contemplation, and by offering an uncluttered stage for rituals of mourning and commemoration, such design may have served psychological needs that we have not fully acknowledged. From the Peace Memorial Park in Hiroshima to Maya Lin's Vietnam Veterans Memorial in Washington and the two pillars of light that pierced the night sky this past spring in lower Manhattan, an austere, reserved aesthetic has been more effective as a vehicle for mourning than most critics of Modernism would care to admit.

Also on display at the Hiroshima Memorial Peace Park is another aesthetic of mourning that has likewise become an "international style" of a different sort. The story of the paper cranes made by Sadako has inspired children and adults around the globe. As most small children now know, Sadako was the young Hiroshima girl who was exposed to radiation at age 2, developed leukemia at 12 and then died before she could finish folding the 1,000 origami cranes she imagined would save her life. When I visited Hiroshima, the park was blanketed with colorful paper cranes, which were heaped by the thousands on park benches and on the sides of buildings and draped on and across sculptures. Unbeknownst to me, an international peace campaign had enlisted people from around the world to send more than a million cranes to Hiroshima between 1996 and 2000. Against the hard, gray-and-white block buildings of the memorial, the brightly colored cranes bore the imprint of children's hands and spoke to a hope for a peaceful world emerging from the ashes of atomic ruin. As I walked around the site, I came across a pile of cranes sent by middle school kids from Littleton, Colorado, the site of the Columbine High School massacre only a few weeks before.

The use of an atomic weapon against Hiroshima marks a turning point in the history of warfare, the transition from wars that took their toll primarily on soldiers to those that routinely ravage civilian populations. Sociologist Charles Tilly has recently argued (in the summer issue of *Boston Review*) that the great, terrible story of twentieth-century violence is the radical increase of civilian death as a percentage of wartime victims. "Over the century as a whole," Tilly writes, "the proportion of war deaths suffered by civilians rose startlingly: according to one estimate, they rose from 5 percent in World War I to 50 percent in World War II, all the way to 90 percent in wars of the 1990s." August 6, 1945, was not the start of this monstrous trend: It had its precursors in the attacks on Guernica, Nanking, Dresden, and Tokyo, and in the Nazis' genocidal war against European Jewry. But Hiroshima made it clear for all to see that humanity had entered a new era of mass killing and civilian suffering—an era that continued through the horrors of Rwanda and Kosovo, the era in which we still live today.

In late September and early October of 2001, I joined other mourners in visits to the makeshift memorials to the WTC attack victims erected in New York's Union Square. The fellow feeling that ennobled human relations in the city immediately after the attacks found expression in that historic space of politics and civic ritual. Flags and patriotic songs, antiwar and antiracist banners, signs demanding vengeance and signs imploring forgiveness, prayer cards, poems and letters written to loved ones and strangers alike, handmade models for monuments, heartbreaking "missing" posters, the intense perfume of scented candles, incense and mounds of flowers, rhythmic drumming by Buddhist monks, performances by Juilliard cellists, and the sounds of quiet weeping briefly claimed the park as a site for collective grief and reflection. Everywhere were images and small-scale replicas of the towers, many sent from the other side of the globe—a fitting tribute to a center for international trade in which citizens of so many countries worked and died. These towers were gifts to a wounded city from people who also knew war and suffering. None were ironic or restrained, none spoke to ambivalence about the towers' design or outlandish scale, none betrayed unease with the government muscle that created them. The buildings stood now as heroic symbols of human resolve, of life against death. Alongside the monuments to this last gesture of Modernist ambition were relics of another kind. The trauma that the loss of the WTC provoked led mourners last fall back to a practice I recognized from Hiroshima. There, amid the xeroxed photos of loved ones, burning incense, poems and prayers, were Sadako's cranes, hundreds and maybe thousands of them—a peace garland laced lovingly across tree branches and through the chain-link fences of the park.

Images and small-scale replicas of the towers were gifts to a wounded city from people who also knew war and suffering.

Civic spaces can begin with mourning, often associated with the efforts of states to enlist the memory of the dead in a national cause. That mobilization of private grief for a national mission continues today: Witness the government's rush to colonize the Washington Mall with a neoclassical World War II memorial that recalls the official architecture of Nazi Germany and Stalinist Russia. Witness, for that matter, the transformation of Washington itself into an armed camp in the weeks after the 9/11 attacks, as huge flags, blocked streets, armed troops and concrete-and-steel barricades turned the center of that city into a war capital. Such mobilization was at odds with the openness and improvisation that reigned briefly in Manhattan's parks and plazas last fall, when the claims of the brokenhearted took precedence over the market and the military. By Thanksgiving, those spaces were cleaned up, their artifacts packed away for safekeeping in archives and museums, and city officials rushed to reassure tourists that New York was again "open for business." The war effort has subsequently seized upon the towers as images of U.S. nationalism, with their silhouette routinely imprinted over the flag in countless posters and bumper stickers. President George W. Bush and other politicians have turned the massacre site into a place for patriotic ceremony and photo-ops. And the tattered flag famously raised from the rubble after the attacks has itself gone on tour to the Olympics and on the space shuttle as an icon of American endurance. The heart of the "I ♥ NY" sticker has been colored red, white and blue, with the nation's embrace of New York threatening to obscure the local and international significance of the tragedy.

But if the recent history of the two Ground Zeros reveals anything, it is that popular mourning in public spaces increasingly reaches across national borders for gestures and rituals resonant with personal and collective meaning. With its austere internationalism, Modernist design may enable such shared mourning and reflection in ways that have eluded both the knee-jerk critics of the Modern movement and its upscale revivalists. Public fascination with the huge fragments of twisted aluminum lying atop the WTC rubble, the temporary "Tribute in Light" memorial and the battered centerpiece of the former WTC plaza, Fritz Koenig's *Sphere* (now relocated to Battery Park), speaks, in part, to the enduring power of abstract form as a shared vocabulary of loss and grieving. The human hand and human heart become visible at such places, where the idealism of abstract art confronts the brokenness born of trauma. We have become so accustomed to the critique of Modernist aesthetics as a false universalism that we have forgotten the spiritual rewards of a stark simplicity. There are times when a common visual language is a necessary resource for a cosmopolitan population drawn from every part of the world, and when a spare, legible landscape is the ideal setting for informal practices that find no home in more identifiably "local" spaces. The mourning of civilians slaughtered in Hiroshima left a legacy that New Yorkers drew on last fall to mourn their own dead. Against the backdrop of two Ground Zeros, Japanese and Americans were united across the decades by the handiwork of children—tiny, fragile birds opening their wings in defiance of horror.

Appendixes

Appendix A: Percent of Persons Who Live in Urban Areas, United States by State (Census 2000)

For Census 2000 the term "Urban Area" refers to both urban clusters and urbanized areas. An urbanized area is an area consisting of a central place(s) and adjacent territory with a general population density of at least 1,000 people per square mile of land area that together have a minimum residential population of at least 50,000 people. (The Census Bureau uses published criteria to determine the qualification and boundaries of urbanized areas.) An urban cluster is a densely settled territory that has at least 2,500 people but fewer than 50,000.

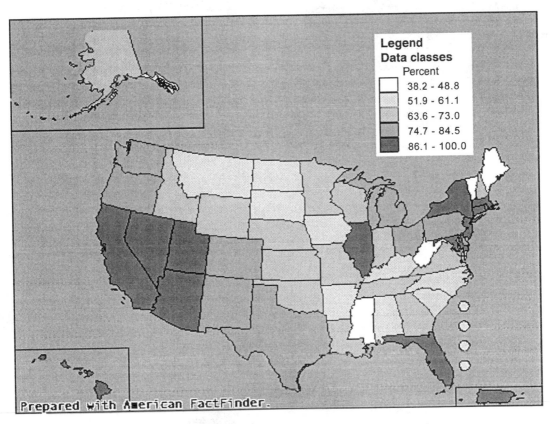

Source: U.S. Census Bureau, *factfinder.census.gov*.

Appendix B: Percent Change in Total U.S. Population from 1990–2000 by State

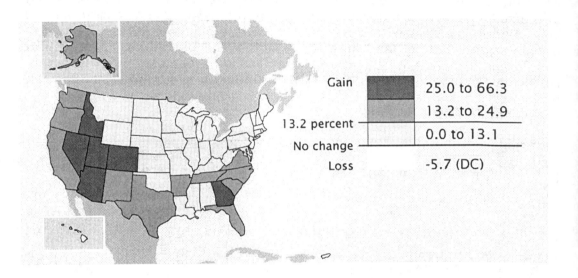

Source: U.S. Census Bureau

Appendix C: Percentage Change in Urban Congestion, 1982 to 1997

From the U.S. Department of Transportation Federal Highway Administration, *www.fhwa.dot.gov*

Large and densely populated metropolitan areas experience increased traffic congestion problems. The cost of traffic congestion to travelers is measured in hours of delay and wasted fuel. Travelers in the nation's 68 largest metropolitan areas spent over $72 billion in hours of lost time and wasted fuel in 1999. Between 1982 to 1997 the annual hours of delay per driver in the country's largest metropolitan areas increased by 125 percent, and in the small urban areas, the average increase was 400 percent. The figure below displays the congestion increases experienced in many urban areas throughout the country.

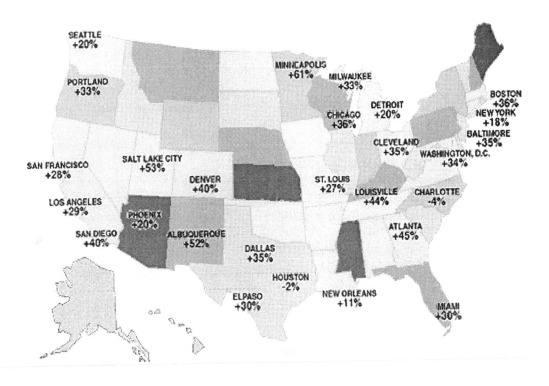

Appendix D: Census Transportation Planning Package (CTPP 2000)

Geographic Area: United States

Subject	Number	Percent
POPULATION		
Total Population	281,421,906	100.0
In households	273,637,396	97.2
In group quarters	7,784,510	2.8
MEANS OF TRANSPORTATION TO WORK		
Workers 16 years and over	128,279,228	100.0
Drove alone	97,102,050	75.7
Carpooled	15,634,051	12.2
Public transportation (including taxicab)	6,067,703	4.7
Bicycle or walked	4,247,479	3.3
Motorcycle or other means	1,043,722	0.8
Worked at home	4,184,223	3.3
TRAVEL TIME TO WORK		
Workers who did not work at home	124,095,005	100.0
Less than 5 minutes	4,180,407	3.4
5 to 9 minutes	13,687,604	11.0
10 to 14 minutes	18,618,305	15.0
15 to 19 minutes	19,634,328	15.8
20 to 29 minutes	25,172,296	20.3
30 to 44 minutes	23,703,903	19.1
45 or more minutes	19,098,162	15.4
Mean travel time to work (minutes)	25.5	(X)

(X) Not applicable
Source: U.S. Census Bureau. Census of Population and Housing, 2000 long-form (sample) data.

Geographic Area: Dallas County, Texas

Subject	Number	Percent
POPULATION		
Total Population	2,218,899	100.0
In households	2,185,365	98.5
In group quarters	33,534	1.5
MEANS OF TRANSPORTATION TO WORK		
Workers 16 years and over	1,038,779	100.0
Drove alone	777,372	74.8
Carpooled	167,270	16.1
Public transportation (including taxicab)	36,925	3.6
Bicycle or walked	18,739	1.8
Motorcycle or other means	10,095	1.0
Worked at home	28,378	2.7
TRAVEL TIME TO WORK		
Workers who did not work at home	1,010,401	100.0
Less than 5 minutes	16,230	1.6
5 to 9 minutes	74,061	7.3
10 to 14 minutes	123,135	12.2
15 to 19 minutes	158,145	15.7
20 to 29 minutes	224,893	22.3
30 to 44 minutes	256,044	25.3
45 or more minutes	157,893	15.6
Mean travel time to work (minutes)	26.9	(X)

(X) Not applicable
Source: U.S. Census Bureau. Census of Population and Housing, 2000 long-form (sample) data.

Geographic Area: Boston city, Suffolk County, Massachusetts

Subject	Number	Percent
POPULATION		
Total Population	589,141	100.0
In households	554,018	94.0
In group quarters	35,123	6.0
MEANS OF TRANSPORTATION TO WORK		
Workers 16 years and over	278,463	100.0
Drove alone	115,618	41.5
Carpooled	25,662	9.2
Public transportation (including taxicab)	89,906	32.3
Bicycle or walked	39,028	14.0
Motorcycle or other means	1,656	0.6
Worked at home	6,593	2.4
TRAVEL TIME TO WORK		
Workers who did not work at home	271,870	100.0
Less than 5 minutes	5,125	1.9
5 to 9 minutes	16,870	6.2
10 to 14 minutes	25,955	9.5
15 to 19 minutes	36,189	13.3
20 to 29 minutes	58,091	21.4
30 to 44 minutes	77,861	28.6
45 or more minutes	51,779	19.0
Mean travel time to work (minutes)	28.8	(X)

(X) Not applicable
Source: U.S. Census Bureau. Census of Population and Housing, 2000 long-form (sample) data.

Bibliography

Books

Bacon, Edmund N. *Design of Cities*. New York: Viking Press, 1967.

Calthorpe, Peter. *The Next American Metropolis: Ecology, Community, and the American Dream*. New York: Princeton Architectural Press, 1993.

Caro, Robert A. *The Power Broker: Robert Moses and the Fall of New York*. New York: Knopf, 1974.

Carson, Rachel. *Silent Spring*. Cambridge, Mass.: Riverside Press, 1962.

Cronon, William. *Nature's Metropolis: Chicago and the Great West*. New York: W.W. Norton, 1991.

Cullingworth, J. Barry. *Planning in the USA: Policies, Issues, and Processes*. New York: Routledge, 1997.

Dreier, Peter et al. *Place Matters: Metropolitics for the Twenty-First Century (Studies in Government and Public Policy)*. Lawrence, Kan.: University Press of Kansas, 2001.

Duany, Andres, Elizabeth Plater-Zyberk, and Jeff Speck. *Suburban Nation: The Rise of Sprawl and the Decline of the American Dream*. New York: North Point Press, 2000.

Garreau, Joel. *Edge City: Life on the New Frontier*. New York: Doubleday, 1991.

Garvin, Alexander. *The American City: What Works and What Doesn't*. New York: McGraw-Hill, 1996.

Grogan, Paul S., and Tony Proscio. *Comeback Cities: A Blueprint for Urban Neighborhood Revival*. Boulder, Colo.: Westview Press, 2000.

Hall, Peter Geoffrey. *Cities of Tomorrow: An Intellectual History of Urban Planning and Design in the Twentieth Century*. Cambridge, Mass.: Blackwell Publishers, 1996.

Hayden, Dolores. *The Power of Place: Urban Landscapes as Public History*. Cambridge, Mass.: MIT Press, 1995.

Jackson, Kenneth T. *Crabgrass Frontier: The Suburbanization of the United States*. New York: Oxford University Press, 1985.

Jacobs, Allan B. *Great Streets*. Cambridge, Mass.: MIT Press, 1993.

Jacobs, Jane. *The Death and Life of Great American Cities*. New York: Random House, 1961.

Katz, Peter. *The New Urbanism: Toward an Architecture of Community*. New York: McGraw-Hill, 1994.

Kay, Jane Holtz. *Asphalt Nation: How the Automobile Took Over America, and How We Can Take It Back*. New York: Crown Publishers, 1997.

Kotkin, Joel. *The New Geography: How the Digital Revolution is Reshaping the American Landscape*. New York: Random House, 2000.

Kunstler, James Howard. *The Geography of Nowhere: The Rise and Decline of America's Man-Made Landscape*. New York: Simon & Schuster, 1993.

Levy, John M. *Contemporary Urban Planning*. Englewood Cliffs, N.J.: Prentice Hall, 1988.

Lynch, Kevin. *The Image of the City*. Cambridge, Mass.: Technology Press, 1960.

Marshall, Alex. *How Cities Work: Suburbs, Sprawl, and the Roads Not Taken*. Austin: University of Texas Press, 2000.

Mumford, Lewis. *The City in History: Its Origins, Its Transformations, and Its Prospects*. New York: Harcourt, Brace & World, 1961.

Orfield, Myron. *American Metropolitics: The New Suburban Reality*. Washington, D.C.: Brookings Institution Press, 2002.

Rusk, David. *Inside Game/Outside Game: Winning Strategies for Saving Urban America*. Washington, D.C.: Brookings Institution Press, 1999.

Whyte, William H. *City: Rediscovering the Center*. New York: Doubleday, 1988.

Wright, Gwendolyn. *Building the Dream: A Social History of Housing in America*. New York: Pantheon Books, 1981.

Web Sites

The following is a list of Web sites for readers who seek more information about issues in urban planning. Due to the Internet's ever-changing nature, the existence of a site is not guaranteed; however, at the time of this publication all Web sites were in existence and operational.

American Planning Association

www.planning.org

A non-profit public interest and research organization, with more than 30,000 members, which is the sponsor of the *Journal of the American Planning Association*. The Web site provides comprehensive information about all aspects of planning and development, plus information about APA events, news, and publications.

ArchNewsNow

www.archnewsnow.com

Comprehensive coverage of national and international news, projects, products, and events in the world of architecture and design.

The Brookings Institution Center on Urban and Metropolitan Policy

www.brookings.edu / urban

This Web site sponsored by the Brookings Institution offers articles and policy briefs about issues affecting urban and metropolitan regions.

Congress for the New Urbanism

www.cnu.org

A San Francisco-based non-profit organization that is considered the leading advocate for the New Urbanist movement. The Web site includes an explanation of NU, information about NU projects, news, event listings, and other resources.

Cyburbia

www.cyburbia.org

Offers a comprehensive directory of Internet resources about urban planning, in addition to message boards, a photo gallery, and news articles.

U.S. Department of Housing and Urban Development (HUD)

www.hud.gov

Provides information about HUD grants and programs, such as public housing and community development, in addition to numerous resources for renters and homeowners.

Knowledge Plex
www.knowledgeplex.org

A Web portal covering issues in affordable housing and community development. Supported by the Fannie Mae Foundation, the site includes news updates, commentary, policy studies, how-to guides, and scholarly reports.

Metropolis Magazine
www.metropolismag.com

The online version of *Metropolis Magazine*, the Web site examines contemporary life through design issues, with a focus on architecture, interior design, product design, graphic design, crafts, planning, and preservation.

National Geographic: New Suburb? Sprawl vs. "Smart Growth"
www.nationalgeographic.com / earthpulse / sprawl

An Internet presentation of a virtual "Smart Growth" neighborhood, created by National Geographic, which provides a visual introduction to the principles of smart growth and New Urbanism. Links to lesson plans are included.

PLANetizen
www.planetizen.com

A comprehensive site featuring daily news updates and editorials about all aspects of urban planning and development, as well as information about jobs and events.

Project for Public Spaces
pps.org / gps

A non-profit organization that offers technical assistance, education, and research to create and sustain public places that are vital to communities, such as parks, plazas, and central squares; buildings and civic architecture; transportation; and public markets.

Sierra Club Sprawl Page
www.sierraclub.org / sprawl

Contains reports and activist resources on sprawl, smart growth, transportation, and livable communities.

Smart Growth Online
www.smartgrowth.org

A Web-based catalogue of news, events, and resources about smart growth. The Web site is a subset of *www.sustainable.org* and receives funding from the U.S. Environmental Protection Agency.

Smart Growth America
www.smartgrowthamerica.com

A nationwide coalition of organizations advocating smart growth. The Web site contains information and resources for promoting smart growth.

Sprawl City
www.sprawlcity.org

A Web site featuring articles and information about the causes and effects of urban sprawl.

UrbanFutures.org
www.urbanfutures.org

A program of the Reason Public Policy Institute. The Web site provides market-oriented analyses of land use and economic development issues.

Additional Periodical Articles with Abstracts

More information on urban planning can be found in the following articles. Readers seeking a more comprehensive selection are advised to consult *Readers' Guide to Periodical Literature*, *Readers' Guide Abstracts*, the *Social Sciences Abstracts*, and other H.W. Wilson publications.

Urban Trees. Roger K. Lewis. *American Forests*, v. 103 pp22–25 Summer 1997.

Lewis argues that trees afford substantial benefits to urban areas. Urban trees provide cityscape ornamentation and frequently much-needed architectural mitigation. By shading streets, sidewalks, plazas, lawns, and gardens, trees provide physiological comfort, and their presence exerts a beneficial psychological effect on people. Trees also shade buildings, thereby decreasing summer air-conditioning and conserving energy. Lewis further explains that, due to their dense foliage, trees can behave as natural screens to dissipate noise, block wind, and provide privacy. Trees have a crucial impact on the natural environment by absorbing moisture and carbon dioxide and emitting oxygen. Furthermore, Lewis writes, trees serve as a habitat for urban wildlife and contribute to soil and water conservation by slowing the amount of water runoff and reducing erosion. In urban areas, trees also represent an economic resource by increasing the value of residential property.

An Urbanist Says a Sense of Place Is More Important than the Design Itself (Interview with Fred Kent). Andrea Oppenheimer Dean. *Architectural Record*, v. 188 pp63–64 April 2000.

Dean presents an interview with Fred Kent, president of the Project for Public Spaces and a follower of the principles of influential urbanist William H. Whyte, who studied the city by observing how people utilize streets and plazas. Topics discussed include the revival of interest in public space, mistakes that architects make when designing public spaces, and the elements that make a space successful.

Architects Are Neglecting the Bulk of Housing Consumers, Causing a Dearth of Good Design and a Rift in the Profession. Andres Duany. *Architectural Record*, v. 187 p22 April 1999.

Duany asserts that architects are failing to cater to the majority of housing consumers. The consumer housing market, which desperately needs new talent, is an area in which good architecture could thrive. Architects' neglect of most housing customers is resulting, however, in a lack of good design and a schism in the profession. Duany argues that these consumers' needs have to be met if architects are to avoid ignoring a massive portion of the built environment.

Where Are We Now? Architecture's Place in an Era of Evolving Values. James S. Russell. *Architectural Record*, v. 191 pp88–92+ March 2003.

The writer discusses architecture's role in an age of changing values in the United States. In buoyant economic times, it mattered less that people thought architecture lacked legitimacy as a means of cultural expression. It has been hoped that the dramatic, sensuous, and even beautiful architectural form-making that has characterized ambitious institutions in America might establish a broader public constituency for design. As Russell reports, while anecdotal evidence suggests that more communities recognize the value of structures that offer amenity to their users and enhance their surroundings, economic uncertainty creates pressure to abandon more graceful designs. Russell asserts that this may be the time for courage, when money and the best of planning should be invested in schools, transportation, housing for those who need it, and public places that both epitomize Americans' ability to work together and help each other and express what they share.

Divided We Sprawl. Bruce Katz and Jennifer Bradley. *Atlantic Monthly*, v. 284 pp26+ December 1999.

Katz and Bradley write that the image of America's cities has dramatically improved in recent years due to the development of downtown areas, but this hides a sometimes horrible reality. In many cases, cities have lost population and economic status throughout the 1990s. From 1990 to 1997, the rate of population growth in America's suburbs was over twice that of its central cities, and even growing cities are unable to keep pace with suburban growth. Urban poverty rates are twice that of suburbs, and the implementation of welfare reform seems to pose a special problem for cities. According to the writers, American cities are losing ground because they push out the people who have choices. Ways in which federal, state, and local policies on spending, taxes, and regulation increase the attractiveness of the suburbs, putting cities at a disadvantage, are discussed. The metropolitan view of American cities is also examined.

Smart Highway. Chana R. Schoenberger. *Forbes*, v. 165 pp290+ March 20, 2000.

Schoenberger reports that Boston is depending on an intelligent transportation system (ITS) to keep traffic in its Central Artery Tunnel moving safely and efficiently. Both the federal government and the state of Massachusetts are spending $12 billion on the Big Dig project, the centerpiece of which is an eight-to-ten-lane subterranean highway that includes interchanges and 14 exit ramps. Schoenberger explains that the $250 million ITS—which consists of digital cameras, vehicle sensors, databases, and fiber-optic links—will serve as a watchdog for road trouble. An ITS-wired road can reduce commuting time by 10 to 45 percent, according to the Federal Highway Administration, and it can identify problems within 2 minutes and have emergency services on the scene within 15.

Smart Air. Tom Arrandale. *Governing*, v. 13 p88 July 2000.

Arrandale reports that the U.S. Environmental Protection Agency has taught Atlanta and its fast-growing suburbs intimidating lessons on the environmental consequences of sprawling development. In 1998 the EPA moved to withhold hundreds of millions of dollars in federal transportation funding because the 13-county Atlanta metropolitan area persistently violated the federal Clean Air Act's ground-level ozone standard. Desperate to keep money for highway projects, the Georgia legislature empowered Governor Roy Barnes to establish and enforce the most far-reaching regional growth-management strategy in America. Earlier this year, the EPA rewarded Georgia by approving its improved clean-air plan. The writer examines how the EPA is enforcing the Clean Air Act in other cities.

Subsidizing Blight. Christopher Swope. *Governing*, v. 15 pp34–36+ May 2002.

Swope discusses how, although the federal government's Section 8 housing program—the housing choice vouchers program—seeks to deconcentrate poverty, it often creates new ghettos. The Department of Housing and Urban Development says families can use vouchers to migrate out of poor neighborhoods and into places with better schools and more jobs, but options are actually limited to a few low-income and transitional neighborhoods. One such area is Patterson Park in Baltimore, which is experiencing an influx of hundreds of voucher holders, many of them from the high-rise public housing Baltimore started demolishing seven years ago. According to Ed Rutkowski, head of a local community development corporation, Section 8 is a catalyst in neighborhood deterioration and ghetto expansion. In his view, the program reconcentrates poverty in struggling neighborhoods, destabilizing an area or even driving out middle-class residents and creating a slum.

Countering Sprawl with Transit-Oriented Development. Dena Belzer and Gerald Autler. *Issues in Science and Technology*, v. 19 pp51–58 Fall 2002.

The authors argue that the incorporation of public transit into planning can help promote efficient land-use patterns and develop a more balanced set of transportation options. Despite some encouraging trends, a need still exists for concerted policy efforts for reshaping land-use patterns at the regional, local, and neighborhood levels, expanding transportation options, and, most importantly, better integrating transportation and development. The writers examine how the need to foster such integration is leading to increasing interest in transit-oriented development (TOD), which concentrates on improving the physical and functional links of transit systems with the surrounding development. Unfortunately, most of the existing so-called TOD projects have failed to realize the full potential of the concept. To articulate a vision of what is possible under TOD, Belzer and Autler write, concrete objectives, research into ways of achieving those objectives, and mechanisms for holding projects to measurable standards are required.

Preserving the Urban Dynamic. Roberta Brandes Gratz. *The Nation*, v. 272 pp22–23 April 23, 2001.

Gratz writes that cities that object to new malls and superstores are enjoying regeneration. The recent defeat of a proposed IKEA superstore in New Rochelle, a small city in a New York suburb, symbolizes a significant turning point in the struggle of communities against the intrusion of big-box retailers. Other big projects that likewise undermine authentic urban places are breaking down in the face of powerful civic resistance. According to Gratz, such defeats are a sign of a positive direction in the regeneration of downtowns. Collapsed projects in Pittsburgh, New Haven, and Baltimore mark the potential end of decades of highly subsidized, developer-driven, national-chain-based projects replacing desolate downtowns that are nonetheless rich in local history, character, and small businesses.

Urban Sprawl. John G. Mitchell. *National Geographic*, v. 200 pp48–73 July 2001.

Mitchell explains that new generations of Americans are looking for living space, giving rise to places plagued by traffic jams, high taxes, and pollution. Known as urban sprawl, the process gobbles up the land, skewers the fabric of community life, and erodes the economic base of older towns and central cities. Outward growth occurs when a city ages and crime and other urban problems motivate many affluent residents to move out. Urban sprawl is claiming farmland, forest, and other undeveloped land at a net annual rate of 2 million acres. An alternative to sprawl, Mitchell suggests, is smart growth, which rests on the assumption that sprawl can be curbed by building better kinds of new communities, fixing up and filling in the old ones, finding ways of encouraging walking instead of driving, and preserving large tracts of open space.

Growing the Inner City? Tamar Jacoby and Frederick F. Siegel. *The New Republic*, v. 221 pp22–27 August 23, 1999.

The authors discuss President Clinton's "third way" poverty program, which amounts to a package of federal tax cuts and loan guarantees designed to encourage private investment in run-down neighborhoods. His proposals reflect a new consensus across the political spectrum that the solution to poverty is capitalism. The idea in this case is that corporations will avail themselves of a forgotten pool of workers, while mainstream investors and local entrepreneurs together create an improved local economy. The writers discuss the record of economic and social development in Harlem, New York, where a 15-year experiment with a similar private-public program has produced mixed results.

'90s Suburbs of West and South: Denser in One, Sprawling in Other.
David Firestone. *New York Times*, ppA1+ April 17, 2001.

Firestone notes that an analysis of the latest census figures shows that the
internal migration to the suburbs that has transformed the United States in
the last 50 years began to slow in the 1990s. Suburbs in the western United
States reached urban-level densities. Suburbs in the southern states detached
themselves from cities and became free-floating patches of population density
tethered loosely to interstate highways. Some suburban outposts established
themselves outside the orbit of big metropolitan areas, while older suburbs
matured into cities, Firestone explains.

Cities Are Fostering the Arts as a Way to Save Downtown. Bruce
Weber. *New York Times*, pA1+ November 18, 1997.

Weber reports that cities around the U.S. are aggressively using the arts as a
way to fuel growth. Cities have created arts districts, financed arts festivals,
and promoted regularly scheduled cultural events.

Razing the Vertical Ghettos. Sarah Downey and John McCormick. *Newsweek*, v. 135 pp36–37 May 15, 2000.

The authors discuss the plans of Chicago mayor Richard M. Daley to save the
city's squalid public housing. Daley wants to demolish all of the city's 58 "family high-rises," including the Robert Taylor Homes, Cabrini Green, and other
crime-ridden failures, as part of a comprehensive plan to replace or renovate
25,000 of Chicago's occupied public housing units, relocating half of the
131,000 legal tenants and an untold number of squatters. The authors report
on the city's difficult dealings with the U.S. Department of Housing and
Urban Development, as well as other complications of the project.

Is Regional Government the Answer? Fred Siegel. *The Public Interest*,
pp85–98 Fall 1999.

Siegel critiques the notion that larger regional governments offer a solution to
urban sprawl in the United States. It is argued that such governments will
exercise a monopoly on land-use decisions, based on the belief that sprawl is
produced when individuals and townships seek to maximize their own advantage without regard for the good of the whole community. Regionalism can
curb sprawl and integrate and sustain central-city populations, Siegel
explains, if it reforms misguided policies and politics that have sent the middle class streaming out of cities. In addition, regional cooperation between the
sprawling high-tech suburbs and the central cities could modernize cities at
risk of being left behind by today's economy. Nonetheless, regionalism is
stronger in logic than in practice. The writer examines why regionalism is not
a panacea for sprawl, referring to the efforts of a number of U.S. cities to
revive inner cities and counter sprawl.

One-Shop Stopping. Nick Gillespie. *Reason*, v. 27 pp37–44 May 1995.

Gillespie reports on the burgeoning anti-superstore movement afoot in the U.S. Opponents of mega-retailers charge that discount chains such as Wal-Mart and Home Depot destroy communities by hounding local merchants out of business and promoting a shallow "drive-by culture." Over the past few years, activists have opposed—sometimes successfully—plans for new super-stores in several different states. For them, there is no such thing as creative destruction—the never-ending process by which market-based societies renew themselves. Instead of considering the good things markets deliver, such as lower prices and greater variety and quality, they instead dwell on the bank-ruptcies, the dislocations, and the difficulties in keeping up. The basic point that the anti-superstore activists fail to address, Gillespie asserts, is that peo-ple like to shop at these stores.

The Science of Smart Growth. Donald D.T. Chen. *Scientific American*, v. 283 pp84–91 December 2000.

Chen writes that widespread concerns about urban sprawl have unleashed a wave of innovation. A recent Pew Center opinion poll found that, of all local issues, Americans are most worried about sprawl and traffic. Indeed, commu-nities are rebelling against the conventional wisdom that continued sprawl is desirable, immutable, and inevitable. The response has been a search for alternatives, often referred to as smart growth. As Chen explains, the term encompasses a range of measures intended to encourage development that offers transportation options, preserves open space, and revitalizes older com-munities. Some of these measures are described, with examples.

Cities in the Next Century. Leonard I. Ruchelman. *Society*, v. 38 pp33–38 November/December 2000.

In part of a cover story on 21st-century living spaces, Ruchelman discusses the future of cities. Largely motivated by advances in transportation and commu-nications, America's urban areas are experiencing an intense restructuring, heralding profound alterations in how the majority of Americans live and work. According to Ruchelman, cities lacking all or some of the important fea-tures that might allow them to fully participate in the global economy are lia-ble to become increasingly left out of the principal growth-promoting economic processes. In the fight to uphold a viable economic foundation, such cities will try to restructure their economies through the formation of such niche mar-kets as tourism, gambling casinos, convention centers, or back-office opera-tions. Areas that have difficulty adapting will have to deal with disinvestment, job losses, and fiscal problems.

Cities That Work. Brendan I. Koerner. *U.S. News & World Report*, v. 124 pp26–33+ June 8, 1998.

Koerner writes about cities that have implemented urban-renewal programs. Despite some positive recent trends, including declining crime rates and balanced municipal budgets, American cities are hindered by the fact that middle-class families continue to leave, and urban poverty has increased. Koerner also looks at a number of cities worldwide that have fostered urban renewal.

It's Time to Reconsider Oppressive Zoning. George W. Liebmann. *USA Today*, v. 125 pp62–63 July 1996.

Liebmann argues that individuals should be permitted to use a small part of their dwelling for gainful employment that does not alter the nature of the surrounding residential area. Many urgent societal problems, including homelessness, social isolation of the elderly, and inadequate child care, can be attributed to zoning restrictions. Modification of local laws to allow accessory apartments, home occupations, and convenience shops in residential areas is compatible with the aims of zoning: protection of residential neighborhoods against traffic, noxious uses, and strangers. Moreover, Liebmann asserts, a society that proclaims respect for private property, self-reliance, and a suspicion of unnecessary government regulation should pause before denying individuals and families free recourse to what is generally the only available buffer against personal, social, and economic dislocations.

Bigger Is Not Better: The Virtues of Decentralized Local Government. Sam Staley. *USA Today*, v. 121 pp10–15 March 1993.

In an article based on a Cato Institute policy analysis, Staley argues that the urban and community development problems suffered by cities can be solved by means of the decentralization and fragmentation (D&F) of government. Regionalists—people who advocate the consolidation of city and county government functions—argue that D&F compromises the ability of cities to compete successfully in the global environment and that the provision of public services and coordinating programs is more efficient through monopoly governments. Their solution, however, is likely to exacerbate existing problems, Staley claims. D&F, on the other hand, encourages free-market solutions to community needs and fosters innovative new services and products. The changing climate of politics and economics in America; the emergence of edge and ring cities; D&F's effect on urban transportation, crime and police work, and neighborhood revitalization; and four policies necessary to make D&F work are discussed.

Land of the Free—Parking. Alan Durning. *Utne Reader*, pp26–29 September/October 2001.

Durning argues that free parking is a major cause of America's insatiable thirst for gasoline and automobile use. He writes that as a nation, we pay more to store our vehicles during the 23 hours a day when they are not in use than we do to keep their tanks full. Fifty percent of the cost of parking is paid by employers, businesses, and taxpayers, and another 40 percent is paid through rent and mortgages for off-street parking at home. Pay parking is rare outside the center of large cities because archaic provisions in zoning and tax codes, along with auto-focused street designs, swell the parking supply and glut the market. According to Durning, the ensuing oceans of parking give workers and customers a big incentive to drive, and dissuade transit, bike, and pedestrian travel by interposing huge parking lots between streets and buildings and by dispersing the places people want to reach. The urge for gasoline and automobile use drives a range of national concerns: rising fuel prices, global climate change, reliance on foreign oil, tightening traffic snarls, relentless sprawl, and worsening urban smog.

A Tale of Two (or More) Downtowns. Jay Walljasper. *Utne Reader*, pp16–17 January/February 2003.

Walljasper explains that planners are suggesting that vibrant cities may need many active centers. A recent conference sponsored by the Center for Architecture in New York, emphasizing the redevelopment of New York after the terrorist attacks of September 11, 2001, delved into the "small is beautiful" notion of spreading new development throughout the city's five boroughs. These urban theorists paint a picture of vibrant urban areas which include a combination of offices, housing, shops, theaters, restaurants, music clubs, museums, and public plazas joined together in the middle of bustling street life at a number of locations around town.

Index